Whispers
FROM THE THRONE ROOM

Reflections on the Manifest Presence

By Steve Porter

WHISPERS FROM THE THRONE ROOM

Reflections on the Manifest Presence

Whispers from the Throne Room
Copyright © 2011 Steve Porter
2nd Edition © 2021 Steve Porter

All Rights Reserved. No part of this publication may be reproduced, stored in a retrieval system, or transmitted in any form or by any means– electronic, mechanical, photocopy, recording or any other –except for brief quotations in printed reviews, without the
prior permission of the author.

All Scripture quotations, unless otherwise specified, are from the King James Version of the Bible (Copyright © 1977, 1984, Thomas Nelson Inc., Publishers.)

Scriptures marked NIV are from the New International Version of the Bible (Copyright © 1973, 1978, 1984, International Bible Society. Used by permission of Zondervan Bible Publishers. All rights reserved.)

Deeper Life Press

Dedicated to my daughters, Alyssa and Britney. I pray your love will grow for the **manifest presence of God** and that long after I am gone the words of this book will continue to live on in your hearts. I pray that God would use you both in powerful ways to bring healing and glory to the nations.

I love you both so much!

♥

Dad

Also dedicated in 2021 to all my future grandchildren with LOVE.

"He who has My commandments and keeps them, it is he who loves Me. And he who loves Me will be loved by My Father, and I will love him and *manifest Myself to him*" (John 14:21).

Acknowledgments

I would first like to thank my lovely wife Diane who encouraged me in this project. Each time I wrote a reflection I would come to her, often choking up as I read. And she never laughed but listened intently.

I would like to thank the late Wade Taylor, my spiritual father of twenty-three years until his graduation to Heaven in 2012, who imparted many of the truths presented here, and also for allowing me to use the writings of Walter Beuttler in the first edition of this book, published in 2011. The new revised and expanded edition of *The Manifest Presence of God* by Walter Beuttler is now available on its own.

I would like to thank my editors Nancy Arant Williams and the late Marie Lawson who made this manuscript shine! Thank you also Marie who encouraged me to get moving to finish this book and for mentoring me in writing and poetry!

A special thank you with appreciation to Connie Daccurzio for proofreading and editing this latest 2021 edition of the book.

Lastly and most importantly, I thank my beautiful Savior who whispered these reflections into my ear.

TABLE OF CONTENTS

Acknowledgments 5
Forward *by Wade Taylor*... 11
Introduction 15
Preface...19
    Taking a Walk with Jesus 33
    The Secret Garden of the Lord... 36
    The Invitation to Walk 38
    The Night Visitor..41
    A Holy Feast 47
    The Manifest Presence of the Lord 49
    The Manifest Presence of Lord (2) 52
    He Stands and Waits... 55
    Footsteps of the Flock 58
    The Word of the Lord...61
    The Word of the Lord (2) 63
    The Word of the Lord (3) 65
    Spirit of Prophecy 68
    Impartation 70
    Amish Farmer 72
    To Sigh after God 76
    Daddy's Girl.. 78
    All Night Prayer..81
    Sin is a Mirage.. 84
    The Beautifully Adorned Bride.. 87
    Building a House of Devotion 93

Streams in the Desert	100
Under the Apple Tree	102
Faithfulness	105
Enoch's Walk	108
Simplicity	113
Valley of Decision	116
Religion is a Dead-end Road	118
Quest to know God	123
Brokenness	127
Tokens of His Communication	130
Mountain of the Lord	132
The Cathedral of my Soul (1)	137
The Cathedral of my Soul (2)	139
Purify Me in Your Presence	141
"The New Reformers"	143
The Angels that Gather (1)	147
The Angels that Gather (2)	150
The Wilderness Way	153
Focus	155
Comparing	159
Climbing Higher (1)	163
Climbing Higher (2)	165
Climbing Higher (3)	167
Sitting Before the Lord	169
Here Comes My Beloved	173
Tears at His feet	175
Fragrance	178

Even unto Death I will Love You...	182
Fellowship of His Sufferings	186
Chambers of Prayer	189
Contagious Prayer	192
Desperate Prayer 1	194
Desperate Prayer 2	196
He Knows My Name!	201
He Knows My Name! (2)	203
Why Can't We Be Quiet?	205
Dew of the Night	207
Affections of the Heart	209
Submitted Lover	211
One Glance from His Eyes	214
A Beautiful Heart	217
Glorious Within	219
Beautiful In Spirit	221
Beautiful In Heart	228
How Will You Be Remembered? (1)	230
How Will You Be Remembered? (2)	234
The Whisper of God	238
Manifest	242
Being Lifted into a Higher Realm	245
Until Tomorrow	250
My Lord	252
Bonus section *Prayers of the Heart*	253
The Lifting	254
Re-Clothe Me	255

Captivate 256

I Press 256

Extravagant Love 257

Release Movement 257

Let Me Love 258

Pen of a Skillful Writer 258

I Want to Be a Son 259

Pearl of Great Price 259

Hear My Prayer 260

We Invite You to Come in and Rest in Our Secret Garden of Prayers 260

Footsteps 261

The Table 262

Spiritual Capacity 262

Draw Me 263

Full Bloom 264

No Other Name 264

Throw Yourself Into His Arms 265

Eye of The Dove 265

The Hidden Revealed 266

Hidden Forest 267

New Beginnings 267

The Fullness 268

About the Author 271

More Books by Steve & Diane Porter 272

Forward
by Wade Taylor

Steve's book *Whispers from the Throne Room*, is not for the faint of heart or for those seeking status quo religion. Its insights emanate from a hungry vessel seeking the very heart of God. Our Lord is calling His people up to a higher level of intimacy at the throne, where they are changed as they enter and abide in His manifested presence.

Surely our "book learning" is valuable. It cannot however, take the place of an experience with God—when we come "face to face" in a personal encounter. Through such personal encounters with the Lord in the life of Steve Porter, this book found its voice. It calls the complacent from passive indifference to a dedicated running after the very heart of God—to embrace a personal touch from a personal Christ that results in a deeper level of revelation in His Manifest Presence.

All the dealings and struggles of life, along with the chastening and scourging we experience, are in reality, preparation for this revelation of the *"manifested glory of the Lord"* throughout our lives.

Paul said, **"I press toward the mark for the prize of the high calling of God in Christ Jesus"** (Phil. 3:14). The goal that Paul is pressing toward is his placement (level of attainment) in the kingdom. He understood that he had to be made ready for this elevation.

> **"I follow after, if that I may apprehend that for which also I am apprehended of Christ Jesus"** (Phil. 3:12b).

> **"Let us be glad and rejoice, and give honor to Him: for the marriage of the Lamb is come, and His wife has made herself ready"** (Rev. 19:7).

Jesus ascended in glory, and He is increasingly releasing and imparting that glory, especially in these last days.

> **"But we all, with open face beholding as in a glass the glory of the Lord, are changed into the same image from glory to glory, even as by the Spirit of the Lord"** (II Cor. 3:18).

This "*open face*" is the result of the "*veil*" having been "*rent*" when Jesus died on the cross, so we can again enter the manifest presence of the Lord. The reason we behold "*as in a glass*" the glory of the Lord, is that this "*glass*" acts as a "*shield*" allowing us to experience as much glory as we can handle. As our capacity increases, the level of the glory we experience will also increase.

The Apostle Paul was on his way to persecute the Church when the Lord suddenly appeared before him in such glory that he fell from his horse and was blinded. This manifestation of glory was so great, Paul had to be prayed for to restore his sight. Much of what he later said of his *pressing toward the mark* may have been due to the never forgotten manifestation of glory the apostle had experienced. And he continually sought to experience again this higher level of glory.

We are living in the last days, and the Lord is preparing a people, calling, "*Come My beloved, let us go forth.*" This is Prophet Ezekiel's "*wheel within the wheel,*" our lives merged into His life that we may become the expression of His life to significantly affect all mankind. There are forerunners whom the Lord is preparing, who will greatly impact the church of our day. Steve Porter is one of these forerunners.

Our world is hastening toward the greatest divine visitation this world has ever witnessed and it is even now being orchestrated. There is a two-fold purpose—the calling out of a people into an end-time cooperative relationship with the Lord, and the ensuing judgments upon the nations. It all begins through the functioning of this "wheel within the wheel." **"The appearance of the wheels and their work was like to the color of a beryl: and they four had one likeness: and their appearance and their work was as it were a wheel in the middle of a wheel"** (Ezek. 1:16).

This glory is a moving glory. Not only are we cleansed and purified in glory, (Isaiah 6:5), but we are being changed—*"from glory to glory"* (II Cor. 3:18). This is the *"wheel within the wheel"* that will lead to the establishing of the government of God in the earth.

Steve's most recent work, *Whispers from the Throne Room* is a powerful end-time word for hungry people seeking the manifest presence of the Lord. As you read these profound Spirit-inspired messages, open the gates of your heart, and you too will be changed "from glory to glory."

Sincerely,
Wade Taylor

Introduction

"For this reason, I am reminding you to fan themselves to flames the gift of God that is within you through the laying on of my hands" (2 Tim. 1:6).

The year was 1992. I was attending Pinecrest Bible Training Center, tucked away in the Adirondack Mountains of Salisbury Center, N.Y. As I hurried down the stairs from my dorm one evening, I was again anticipating a few precious minutes with Wade Taylor to receive counsel and prayer. The line at his office door was long, and the wait certain as I fell onto a couch and prepared for the delay. I was accustomed to the long lines every evening to see our Bible college president. The deep hunger inside me told me it would be worth the wait.

Wade Taylor had something special. He had a unique walk with his God, and he carried the Lord's manifest presence. He himself had received a powerful impartation many years ago given by Walter Beuttler, and it was very evident in his ministry. Wade's deeper walk encouraged me to pursue God for myself, to also obtain an abiding manifest presence in my own life.

An hour and fifteen minutes later, I was ushered into his office where he greeted me warmly. I nervously walked to a special spot in his office where he loved to pray for people. He took my hands and prayed, "Give Steve a special anointing to speak from his heart, and a gift to write and communicate." All at once the manifest presence came, and I felt the tangible power of God surge through my arms and body. The prayer was heartfelt, as I sensed the nearness of God in Wade's office that evening.

After thanking him, I left his office. Wade had encouraged me to stay in touch, saying he believed God was active in my life. I climbed the two flights of stairs back to my dorm and entered my room. I fell onto my bed and lay there silent. I could sense the nearness of God as my body still literally vibrated under the power of God. I felt a heat surging through me. A fire was burning through my soul, and I knew I had received fresh impartation.

Then I knelt before the Lord, just basking in His presence. I pledged my very life to Him and asked if I too, could carry the presence of God. The Lord responded by giving me an even deeper hunger for more. This hunger kept me going to Wade Taylor's office, sometimes nightly. I always ended up on my face before the Lord in my dorm room deep in the stillness of the night.

Eighteen years have passed since those special nights at Pinecrest. Yet I vividly remember Wade's mentoring and the flames of fire the Lord fanned in my life when we were together. I remember lying on my face in my dorm savoring the glory of the Lord for hours as I was transformed by the manifest presence of God. Even today, fire for the deeper things of the Spirit still burns inside me, sparked by those times spent with Wade Taylor in prayer. He would pray with me regularly on the phone, and I could sense the nearness of the Father as he prayed.

My prayer is that through this book a fire would also be ignited in your life. I pray that even while reading, His manifest presence would come and that you would have an intimate encounter with a personal Christ. That you would come to love the manifest presence, and you too would hear, "whispers from the throne room." That you would come to know the heart of God and be changed by His GLORY!

Dear precious Lord, please come walking into the room of this dear reader. Let them experience Your manifest presence and be transformed. Let a deep hunger be stirred inside of them, as they are changed from "glory to glory." Jesus, give them a token, the reciprocation of Your love for them by means of the manifest presence. Visit them even now...

If I could sit with you as with a friend, in a warm room by a cozy fire—these are the things I would share from the depths of my heart. I hope you'll feel free to put your feet up and relax as you read on...

Preface

This is perhaps one of the most powerful pieces of writing I have ever read. I can't tell you how many times I have read this, and it brought me to tears as I lay prostrate on the floor in His manifest presence. Gabe Hoffman, the author of this piece, captures the beauty of a true ministry unto the Lord. I knew I had to share this with others as it also captures the very heart of this book. Thank you, Gabe Hoffman, for hearing this whisper from the throne room as it has truly transformed the body of Christ.

With Love and Prayers,
Steve Porter

The Door to God's Heart

by Gabriel Hoffman

I saw the Lord Jesus come to me. He said, "Come, Father has something special for you." Excited, I followed my Lord and Savior to the throne room. Father God was there in all His majestic glory. He greeted me with a smile. "Son," He said, "It is time for you to choose your life and ministry."

"Really?" I responded with joy and amazement. "Oh, Father! This is the day I have been waiting, preparing, and praying for. Is it really time?"

"Yes, My son. It is time. But you must choose wisely, for this will be your life's work."

Then I remembered that He was Lord of my life. "But Father, what is your will for me?" He smiled. "Son, I've prepared you to serve me in any number of ministries. The choice is yours. Truly I give you the freedom to choose from the set of options I have prepared for you. Any of them will please Me as long as you are faithful in how you carry them out. Do you understand?"

"Yes Father." I replied, still too stunned to say anything more. Father took me to a great golden door and led me through. It opened to a corridor curving gently downhill and to the left. In the corridor stood a number of tables, each with an object on it. Beside each table was a door that exited the hallway.

"My dear son," said Father, "We will go to each table and I will explain the ministerial gift and call you may choose. I will answer any questions you have. At any point, you may choose an option and exit through the appropriate door into your ministry and My happiness."

"Yes Father, I am ready to begin." The first table was covered in bright green velvet and held a bottle of oil. Over the doorway was inscribed, "HEALING." I looked questioningly at the Father. "This is the ministry of healing. The green table represents health and life. The bottle is the healing oil of the Holy Spirit. In this ministry you will have power to touch people in spirit, soul and body and bring My healing to many."

I thought to myself, "This would be great! Oh, the aching hearts and broken bodies I could touch. The glory that would be brought to Jesus by this!" Yet, something in my heart tugged at me. "Father! This would be wonderful, but...."
"But I feel you have something even more important for me." He smiled and led me to the

next table. As we walked to the next table, I noticed how the carpet looked worn in front of the door of Healing. I asked Father about this. "Many have chosen this door. Those who were faithful brought great glory to the Kingdom and pleasure to Me. Those who abused the gift brought shame to us and themselves."

The next table was made of electric blue azure. On it laid a wooden staff. Over the doorway was inscribed "MIRACLES" in blazing letters. As we stopped in front of the table, Father spoke. "The blue represents My power. On the table is Elijah's staff. With it you can have tremendous power with man and nature. You can do supernatural acts for Me."

The Staff of Elijah! I had long admired his power, and his mighty exploits for God. And yet, that longing inside my heart was not satisfied. "This would be tremendous, my Lord, but somehow, my heart yearns for something deeper, and more lasting." I thought I caught a glimmer of approval on Father's face as He said, "Very well, shall we go on?"

I nodded. We went around the curved corridor until I could no longer see the door by which we entered. Next, we came to a table of black marble shot through with white. Over the doorway

"PROPHECY" was written in bold block letters on a pure white background. On the table was a worn pair of sandals. As we stopped in front of the table, Father spoke again.

"The colors represent the nature of prophecy. The prophet clearly sets forth the light of the Truth in a world darkened by lies. The sandals belonged to John the Baptist. In this ministry, you would be my oracle to those of the world."

"Prophecy?!" I thought to myself. "That would be outstanding. I've always longed to speak the very words of God. There are so many lies going around the world and even in the Church. There is a desperate need for true prophets in these last days."

Still, the tugging in my heart did not cease. In fact, it grew stronger. Father smiled again in approval.

"Son, you are wise to be thoughtful about these gifts. They are very powerful and can be quite dangerous if pursued with a wrong heart, like carrying a large electric current through a corroded wire. Many have used these gifts well and have entered into My joy, but too many others have destroyed themselves and those around them in their abuse of these gifts. You are free to choose these, and I will work with and in you for their proper use."

"Thank you, Father, but I desire something deeper and closer to Your heart."

"Closer to My heart, son? Very well, let us press on." As we walked farther down the corridor, I noticed two things. First, the light was growing somewhat dimmer and second, I could hear a faint thump-thump in the distance. It sounded like a drum and although I wondered about it, I held my peace.

The next table was made of brightly polished brass. On it laid a finely made trumpet. Over the doorway was written "EVANGELISM" in letters nearly as bright as the sun.

We stopped in front of the table, and I quietly waited for Father to explain this ministry to me. He began speaking. "The ministry of evangelism is very special in the Kingdom.

The brass table represents My judgment against sin. The trumpet heralds the Good News that My Son, Jesus bore the Judgment on behalf of mankind. The brilliant lettering is a glimpse of the Heavenly Kingdom."

I pondered these things silently for a moment. It would be such a thrill to lead others to New Life in Jesus. There are so many suffering people who need the Good News. The Lord Jesus and the

Father deserve to have more people gathered around the Throne in worship and adoration. Does not all of Heaven rejoice each time a sinner repents? I knew that this ministry would bring great joy to the Father, but the tugging on my heart grew stronger.

"Oh Father, this would be truly wonderful, but I feel that you still have something more for me. Father, may we go on?"

"Yes, son. The choice is yours. Let's go to the next table."

We walked farther down the corridor and came to a table made of pure white alabaster.

On it were a piece of slate and chalk. Over the doorway was written "TEACHING."

"Son, this is also a very special ministry to the Kingdom. There are so many in dire need of proper teaching of My true Word, the Word as it is recorded in the scriptures and that which is being poured forth day after day from the throne. The white table represents the purity of the properly taught Word. The slate and chalk represent the instruments of an instructor of the things of God."

This is it, I thought. "This is what I came to Bible School for. I know the Lord has placed a call for teaching on my heart. And, as Father said, it is desperately needed in the body of Christ."

I was just about to tell Father that this was the one I wanted when I felt the tugging even stronger in my heart. I looked down the corridor. It was dark but it seemed like the drumbeat was coming from that direction. It wouldn't hurt to see what else Father had available.

"Father, this is the one that I thought was for me, but now I'm not so sure. Can we walk a little farther?"

"Of course, my son."

As we walked on, I noticed that the light was growing dimmer, and the drum beating was more distinct. I asked Father about it.

"Son, the lights are dimmer here as we descend farther away from the more open and public ministries. As for the drum beating, I think it is best if you discover the source of that for yourself."

We walked farther down the corridor and came to its end. Three tables were set there; one on each side and one at the end. We stopped in front of the table on the right. It was made of pure silver and glimmered, even in the dim light. On it was a small wooden cross. Across the doorway, written in blood red letters, was the word "LOVE."

"This is a deep ministry, my son. Few come this far. The silver represents a pure reflective surface for My love to shine upon. The cross is a symbol of the sacrifice of Jesus, in demonstrating ultimate love to the world. The blood-colored letters are a memorial to the blood shed there."

"Love?" I whispered. "That is what this hurting world needs so incredibly. There are so few who really love with God's true love. It would be a tremendous privilege to carry His love where He bids." Yet, the longing in my heart was still not satisfied.

We turned around to see the table on the left wall. It was made of black ebony. On it was a simple mat. Written above the doorway was the word "INTERCESSION." On the door itself was this question; "Who will stand in the gap?"

The Father spoke quietly. "The black represents the darkness and depth of intercession. It is dark in the prayer closet and an intercessor must be willing to go into the depths of sin to rescue the perishing by prayer. The prayer mat is the simple tool of the intercessor. There are so few intercessors, son. Few people will make themselves so available to Me that they will not despise a work which appears to be nothing while in reality, moves the entire universe."

"Oh Father, to be a true intercessor. To represent man before You and represent You before man. I would so love to be able to stand in the gap and pray your burdens for the world. I know I would receive little earthly recognition. I would be satisfied in knowing that I was part of your touch in this world. But what is the final ministry?"

We walked a short distance to stand before the final table and door. There was very little light, and the drumbeat was quite loud. The table was made of pure gold and shined with an inner light. On the table was a small golden altar with incense burning. Over the doorway was written, in gold letters,

"MINISTRY UNTO GOD"

Father spoke very quietly, barely audible over the drumbeat. "Son, this is a ministry that very, very few choose. The gold represents divinity. The altar is one that stands in the Heavenly tabernacle and burns fragrant incense to Me. This ministry will not earn earthly recognition. The world and most of the Church may think you spend your time for naught. It is the ministry of service to Me, not to achieve anything or affect the world but merely to be My worshipper, companion, and friend."

Father stood there looking quietly at the door. I could not see His face in the dim light. I

asked Him, "Father, what is your desire?"

"Son, you are free to choose any; I rejoice in all faithful service."

So, I stood there quietly thinking. What did I really want to do with my life? There are so many needs in the world and in the Church. So few were truly faithful. I knew the workers were few. And yet, I could not shake the growing desire in my heart. To serve God? Nothing else; just to minister unto Him.

How many others would there be with me? Would my family understand? What about my church?

As I pondered all of this, Ion. Couldn't a few of us start now? Then I thought of all that Jesus had done for me on the cross.

What higher thing could I do with my life, anyway?

"Father, I choose this door, this path." Are you sure, My son?" "Yes Father, quite sure." "Good son, go in."

As Father turned to face me, I could see tears streaming down His face. I stopped in amazement. Before I could think about it, I reached up and wiped His tears. I then realized what I had done.

"Father, please forgive me. I didn't mean to be so impertinent." He reached down and hugged me. "Son, never be sorry for that. You have dried My tears and you will do it many times again in this ministry. There is so much in the world that brings Me to tears of grief. Only a few move Me to tears of joy!"

With that, Father opened the door for me and motioned me to enter. As I went in, the first thing that struck me was the drumbeat. It was quieter in the room. I realized that it was not a drumbeat at all, but His heartbeat. Next, I saw someone coming to embrace me. I knew just by looking at Him that He was Jesus.

Warmly, He said, "It is wonderful to see you here. So you have chosen to minister to the

Father with Myself and the other great people in this room. Slowly, I turned my head. Enoch, Abraham, Moses, Joshua, and many others gazed upon me with welcoming expressions.

"With you? All of you?" I asked bewildered. "Of course! What do you think I was doing for all of eternity before there was any creation? I ministered unto the Father. And now, I'm so glad that you are joining us in this marvelous duty and alliance."

Jesus then turned to me, His expression more serious. "It is time that I give you this precious gift." In His hand was a beautiful ornate golden key. I was puzzled.

Then He said, "This is the key to God's Heart. It allows you to have access to Him at all

times. You see, this is a Master Key. In His house, it will fit all the doors you passed by.

Because you choose Him and ministry to Him, you will be afforded intercession, teaching, evangelism, love and all the other ministries.

For all of the lesser are found in the Greater!

Taking a Walk with Jesus

"And they heard the voice of the LORD God walking in the garden in the cool of the day…" (Gen. 3:8a).

"Enoch walked faithfully with God; then he was no more, because God took him away" (Gen. 5:24).

Come close to the Lord and walk with Him awhile, for He cherishes you and wants nothing more than to spend time with you. His voice is soothing, His countenance is lovely, and His words feed your spirit like nothing else ever could. They refresh your soul and call you deeper into His presence. Oh, the depths of His love for you!

Did you know that you can spend time just walking with your friend Jesus and beholding Him in His glory without saying a single word? Just to open your heart to Jesus and love on Him (Ps. 62:5). The truth is that you can take walks with Him, just admiring and cherishing His presence. On a personal level, some of the most powerful times

I've spent with the Lord have occurred while I was outdoors, spending time alone with God. During those times the Lord comes and reveals Himself to me. The reality is that He will respond to those who deeply love Him without distraction—those who have no agenda but His.

Just as Enoch walked with God in close, intimate fellowship, sharing his heart with his best friend Jesus, I realized that I too could walk with Jesus and share what I am thinking and feeling. I call these times "Enoch walks." I imagined Enoch embracing his kids and family and then picking up a walking stick as the sun was setting and going for a walk with God. I also picked up my stick and took long walks with the Lord every evening just before the sun went down. These "Enoch Walks" transformed my prayer life. In fact, I could picture the Lord walking with me on that beach or in that forest. I sensed that He stood right beside me in all His beauty and splendor. His eyes that blaze with fire were burning with the increasing passion inside me.

We come to God just as we are, hang-ups and all, and quietly walk with Him in His divine presence. In that special place, our heart is still, and we know that He is our God. As we walk with Him day by day, He is changing us even though we sense nothing changing. We continue to hold our hearts open before Him, resting in His loving presence. Intimacy grows slowly at times, but we dare not judge it by how we feel. Rather, we must choose to trust Him, for He is at work in our hearts during those times together. Enjoy anointed worship and let your heart respond in humble adoration. You don't have to say anything, just enjoy walking with Him there in your secret garden. You can do this for hours, knowing He is there with you. I sometimes set out two chairs, one for me and another for Him. There I rest in His tender love. If you lie at His feet on the floor, you may sometimes fall asleep there, but don't worry, beloved, because He loves it when you relax enough to sleep in His arms. As you continue to spend time together, intimacy grows, and you are changed into His likeness.

The Secret Garden of the Lord

Recently in my spirit the Lord gave me a vision so powerful it literally changed my life. It stirred me so deeply that I commissioned an artist to paint a portrait of it. It hangs on our wall, and we take it with us to meetings where we minister, eager to stir the Bride to a more intimate walk with God.

In my vision I saw the beautiful Bride of Christ standing at the gate of a beautiful secret garden. The garden was lush with greenery and sweetly scented beautiful flowers. As the bride walked through the gate, the sweet Master was already waiting there for her. He was standing there with such love in His eyes, bidding His bride to come closer, to walk with Him in the cool of the evening. It was powerful to watch their affectionate interaction as they walked together. They also had a special bench where they sat together just enjoying each other's presence. Then I heard the lyrics of the beautiful hymn "In the Garden" written by Charles Austin Miles in 1913 (public domain).

I come to the garden alone While the dew is still on the roses
And the voice I hear falling on my ear The Son of God discloses
And He walks with me, And He talks with me And He tells me I am his own
And the joy we share as we tarry there None other has ever known
He speaks and the sound of His voice Is so sweet the birds hush their singing And the melody that He gave to me Within my heart is ringing
And He walks with me And He talks with me And He tells me I am his own
And the joy we share as we tarry there None other has ever known

Can't you feel the sense of peace in the holy garden of God?

The Invitation to Walk

The sweet Heavenly Bridegroom will wait until He finds someone who is willing to walk closely with Him. As we walk with Him, He shares the deep things in His heart, the deep secrets reserved for only His closest friends.

"And they heard the voice of the LORD God walking in the garden in the cool of the day…" (Gen. 3:8a).

The voice of the Lord walking is not a mistype. This speaks of the Lord coming for fellowship in the cool of the evening. He comes when the sun is setting, and the air is now cool and comfortable. Isn't He considerate? Such a good God we serve that He looks out for us this way. The voice of God "walking" expresses that what He is speaking today is beyond the Word that He spoke yesterday, and that which He will reveal tomorrow will be far beyond that which He speaks today.

In our walks with the Lord, we are downloaded with divine revelation that takes us deeper and higher than where we started, but there is still more to come. As we walk with the sweet Master He teaches us the mysteries of God, sharing both His deepest longings and His dearly held secrets.

Can you see the Lord bidding you to come and walk with Him? He has been walking in this garden for thousands of years. The sweet Bridegroom will wait until He finds someone with whom He can walk and share His secrets. The heroes of the Bible walked with the Lord through the lush garden. Enoch and Noah knew the secret of walking with God (Gen. 6:9), as did Abraham (Gen. 24:40). David walked there in the garden where he discovered the courts of the Lord. John the Beloved was in the holy garden of intimacy where he leaned on His Lord. And so can you, but only if you're willing. The door is always open if you choose to enter. There is deep healing for wounds and hurts as you walk with the Healer Himself. As you walk together, He will declare over you, "Behold, I make all things new!"

In this garden of the Lord, the heavenly Bridegroom is waiting for you, His bride, while the dew is still on the roses. As soon as you enter, the Master speaks with such love and tenderness that your heart is moved with pure worship. You walk together and smell the intoxicating scent of flowers as you enter this garden where, with tears, your Bridegroom declares that you belong to Him. You are His dearly beloved, His spotless bride, His beautiful one. His voice is soothing, His countenance is lovely, and His words are like honey to your heart. They refresh your soul and call you deeper into His presence. Oh, the depths of His love for you! Time stands still as even the birds are suddenly quiet, sensing that it is a holy moment. Then the sweet Master sings a song over you, a song of rejoicing over the day you were born. You are moved, you are undone as you linger in such a divine appointment. Your joy is indescribable; in that season your wounds are healed, and your sorrow is turned into dancing! You continue to walk and share heart to heart. You gaze on His beauty, realizing that He is your safe refuge, and you never want to leave that incredible place. Come, dear friend, and walk with your Beloved Savior—you will find Jesus waiting for you in the garden of the Lord where the door is always open just for you.

Oh, Father, may I take a walk with you now? I am so hungry, yearning to touch Your face and dry Your tears as we walk hand in hand in the secret garden of holy communion. Bid me come, dearest Lord Jesus, as I will be waiting for You to approach the gate and meet me in our special place.

The Night Visitor

On May 5, 2006, the Lord gave me this vision as I was waiting on Him during the night season. As they gradually unfolded in front of me, I clearly saw the following events take place.

**I sleep, but my heart is awake; it is the voice of my beloved!
He knocks, saying, "Open for me, my sister, my love, my dove,
my perfect one; for my head is covered with dew,
my locks with the drops of the night"** (Song of Solomon 5:2, NKJV).

Behold, I stand at the door and knock. If anyone hears My voice and opens the door, I will come in to him and dine with him, and he with Me" (Rev. 3:20, NKJV).

As I lay in my bed, I heard the sound of faint knocking. It was **the One** whom my soul loves. My heart leaped within me as He spoke to me saying, *"Come away with me, My love."* He had a special invitation in His hand, rolled like a scroll. I jumped out of bed eager to open the scroll. I quickly read the words, "I have invited you to a feast prepared for you. Will you come?" I said, "Yes, Jesus. I would love to."

"Come right away and bring nothing with you," He said tenderly, as we approached the hallway leading to my living room.

I was glad I had answered His knock that night or I would have missed my invitation to "feast at His table." As I walked with Him into my living room to my favorite prayer chair, my "secret place" was suddenly transformed into a huge dining hall complete with fine china, set perfectly in preparation for the big event. The table was beautifully laid, ready for a special feast.

Jesus took His place at the head of the table. His eyes, so full of love, made me feel welcome. He spoke to me with such tenderness, that "my heart leaped" within as He fixed His gaze on me. There were others who sat at the table, but it was as if Jesus and I were alone in a special place prepared just for us.

My Beloved told me many others were invited to come dine with Him at His table that night, but they would not answer their door to let Him in. I recalled that He had been weeping when I answered the door, overcome to have found a companion with whom to share His heart. At that moment I realized His hair was wet with dew of the night because He had been standing in the cool night air.

I quickly got up off my chair and fell at His feet. "Oh, Precious One," I cried, "how many times have I left You standing all alone out in the night air? How many times have You been *wet with the dew?* Oh, Lord, how many times have I chosen the comfort of my bed instead of time with You? I often made You walk alone into the night with Your heart breaking." My tears fell faster than I could wipe them away. "Get up my child," He said, "I don't remember those times, because they are *under my blood!*"

He gently pulled me off the floor and embraced me. Oh, the love I felt as I leaned against Him. He whispered into my ear, "Thank you for keeping Me company tonight. Only a few of My choicest servants responded to the call *to come.*"

I took my place at the table again. Jesus was excited about the meal He had prepared. He served His divine meal to one person at a time. When He came to me, He served me only a small portion of food and gave me only a little to drink while those around me had plates full and cups overflowing. While I ate with the others, I said nothing, but I was perplexed.

The Lord *perceived what was in my heart* and when everyone had finished the meal He spoke. "Some ask in their hearts why I gave more substance to some, but not to others. "This meal symbolizes the deeper things of God, the very secrets of my heart, and I gave you according to your capacity to receive. As you keep coming to this table I have freely set before you I will enlarge your capacity to receive through your obedience to the knocks at your door. I must tell you, however, that I will come at inconvenient times. I want to know, My dear one, that if you love Me as much as I love you, I will share many secrets with you, but only if you are willing to come. And as I have said before only a few choose to respond to My invitation. Most are tucked comfortably in their beds unwilling to lose sleep...but I am the night visitor."

All at once I was back in my living room with my heart full of **the One** I desired most. His presence lingered. Night after night I heard Him knocking. And while I was asleep my heart was always awake, so I could hear his affectionate call, "Come away with Me, My love." My living room was often transformed into a banquet hall where I sat at His table with my invitation in hand. I joined only a few others; there was never a crowd.

Each night at His table I was served more and greater *substance*. My capacity to receive was growing with every meal. I drank my *new wine*, as my heart overflowed with joy in the "fullness of His presence." I was "intoxicated with His love." I was quite content just to sit quietly with Him.

"You have ravished My heart, my treasure, my Bride," He proclaimed. *"With only one glance of your eyes, you have become to me as a garden enclosed. Eat, O beloved friends. Drink, yes, drink abundantly of My love."*

His eyes were so full of love that my heart was moved as if it was my first visit with Him. From deep within I cried, *I am my Beloved's—the one He desires.* "Come, my love," I pleaded, *"let us go and spend the night together. There will I give you my love."* I woke up the next morning still in His arms and ate while leaning on the chest of my Lord.

Each night as I climb into bed, my heart is always awake, listening ever so closely for that familiar knock from the One I desire more than life itself. I vowed not to leave Him standing outside, all alone in the night. He comes with invitation in hand; my night Visitor has prepared a special place for me. There He shares His heart, uttering whispers from the throne room that can be heard nowhere else, only at His table, where I feast on His presence.

"Many are called but few are chosen" (Matt. 22:14).

Father, I make myself available to You in the night seasons. I sleep but my heart is awake... Speak, Lord, for Thy servant has a listening heart...

A Holy Feast

"You shall have a song as in the night when a holy feast is kept, and gladness of heart, as when one sets out to the sound of the flute to go to the mountain of the LORD, to the Rock of Israel" (Isa. 30:29).

Who are we that God would invite us to spend time with Him during the night hours? When others are tucked away in bed, it is an amazing thing to keep the Lord company. Some of my most precious times with Him have been those nights when I enjoyed a holy feast. The truth is that a holy feast is available to all who will sacrifice their comfort and get up to meet with their God.

There is a school that meets at night. **It is the King's College.** This school requires no money but does require obedience far beyond what is usual. Not many will pay the price. Attending this school may cost them more than they can handle.

Feasting at the Lord's table at night is more rewarding than I can explain in mere words. The truth is that some things are better caught than taught. When you grasp the treasure of feasting on His presence and sitting at His table you will never be the same again.

I am amazed that I would even be allowed to keep the Lord *company* at night—that I could ever touch His heart. Yet, His heart is moved when I attend the *King's College* and sit at His feet to hear His heart, to love on Him, to just be silent, relishing the moment of such holy communion.

Lord, I want to keep You company in the night when others are tucked away in bed. I want to sit up with You and just love on You. I embrace You; I love You, and I want to have a holy feast unto You. I want to be a constant companion of my God!

The Manifest Presence of the Lord

*"Where can I go from Your Spirit? Or where can I flee from Your presence?
If I ascend into heaven, You are there; If I make my bed in hell, behold,
You are there"* (Ps. 139:7-8, NKJV).

We know God has an abiding presence; He is everywhere at the same time. No matter where we are on this earth, He is there! We cannot hide from His presence. Ready or not He is always there. It is comforting to know He stands right beside us. At times He is unnoticed and unseen, yet He stands in the shadows yearning to reveal Himself to those He adores.

Once I went through a really dry season and became very discouraged. I was even questioning my calling! I felt the prophetic voice inside of me was being silenced and knew the devil was responsible. The *enemy of our souls* does not want the people to hear the message of intimacy. Satan well knows if people really caught this message, it would bring about a powerful visitation of the Spirit of God and they would never be the same again. Satan's mission is to keep people in religious bondage. It seemed every time I turned around, I could feel *the adversary* doing his best to silence me, and it broke my heart.

One day I was driving my vehicle down the road, late for an appointment. Suddenly I felt the Spirit of God stirring inside of me. I sensed His desire to meet with me, so I obeyed, parking my car near a recreational area where I got out to walk across the grounds. As soon as I sat down by a tree and placed my hood over my face, His presence came upon me so strongly that I couldn't contain my emotions. As I broke down in tears, I literally felt the Lord come to stand beside me. I didn't see Him with my natural eyes, but I knew He stood to my right.

For some time, I couldn't move because His presence was upon me so powerfully, and I couldn't stop weeping. After a time, I decided I needed privacy, so I returned to my SUV and lay face forward on the back seat where His presence continued to be poured out in me. I knew He had come to let me know He was with me, that He had a plan for my life, and that somehow in His time He would provide a platform for the words He had spoken into my heart. That encounter helped me through some rough days ahead.

This presence I'm speaking of is **His manifest presence.** It is when the Lord reveals Himself as a person with personality and feelings. To experience His manifest presence is to be quickened and renewed with a deep inner contentment, obtained only through experience. His previously intangible presence suddenly becomes tangible and all-consuming when He reveals Himself in a very personal way.

The Lord's *"abiding presence"* is everywhere at the same time. But during His *"manifest presence"* He actually reveals Himself in His glory. Did you know the Lord desires to meet with you in a personal way? He wants to hold you in His arms and ravish you with His love. You can sit together, not necessarily talking a lot, but just being together and sharing what you wouldn't want to share in public or with anybody else. His manifest presence will be made known to you, if you hunger for more than just a casual relationship with Him.

Father, I so desire Your manifest presence. Reveal Yourself to me in a personal way today.

The Manifest Presence of Lord (2)

I suddenly awakened to what I thought was an audible warning siren. I was jolted out of my sleep but heard and saw nothing to prove it had actually happened. A quickening in my spirit told me this was a spiritual warning. I heard it through my "inner ear," but the sound was so loud it woke me. Even now I'm not sure whether it happened in the natural or the spiritual. What I did know was that it was "the sound of the Lord." My good friend Joel Killion said it best: "There is a particular 'sound' which inherently, yet quietly, vibrates within the subtle stillness of God's tangible presence."

"And let it be, when thou *hearest the sound of a gong* in the tops of the mulberry trees, that then thou shalt bestir thyself: for then shall the LORD go out before thee, to smite the host of the Philistines" (2 Sam. 5:24).

This "gong" is the sound of the Lord moving, working His purpose in our midst. And this warning was indeed the sound of the Lord at work and was given to me for a special reason.

I heard the Lord say *"There will be hotspots of My glory."* He then asked me to pray for the West Coast, in particular—California. I sensed that the Lord wanted to bring hotspots of His glory there. I prayed against the enemy's plan for that state, and trusted God for powerful breakthrough. California is not the only area singled out—many other places will have open heavens where His manifest Presence will dwell.

I have never heard the term "hotspots of My glory," until that morning. Although, I'd once seen a vision of a map/grid with several lights on it. I could plainly see towns and cities all represented by a light on the grid. **The Lord said, "In the last days many will be lighthouses that will reflect My glory."**

The Spirit will *"hover over the face of the deep"* at this time and we will reflect His glory like the beautiful reflection of the sunrise glistening over the fresh waters of the Great Lakes. The first time this occurred was when the Creator hovered over the darkness of the deep. Now that the Son dwells within us we have the light of God shining through us. He will use His *city on a hill* to be a *light unto all the world.* We who love and worship Him will be carriers of God's glory.

Can we experience the same intimate atmosphere that we get in the throne room in these hotspots of glory? Does God desire for His manifest presence to invade these hotspots? Yes! God is pouring out His Holy Spirit upon those who are spiritually hungry and filling the spiritually unsatisfied. This is the pre-qualification required to be a "hotspot." He is creating hotspots connected to the throne within the hearts and minds of those who seek Him passionately and without reservation. Many hotspots are already forming. The manifest presence is building.

There are deeper dimensions in God (John 14:2) that we have not yet entered—places in the spirit we have not seen. The manifest presence of the Lord will dwell in those who desire the deeper realms of the spirit. A direct connection to the atmosphere of heaven is being granted to those who have fully committed themselves to loving Him. The Lord wants us to know He is preparing a place and a people to be that "hotspot" to reflect His very **Shekinah Glory.**

Father, my heart desires to see a hotspot of Your glory in my city! Visit our area and transform us, turning our world upside down with Your power and might.

He Stands and Waits...

"My beloved is like a roe or a young hart: behold, he standeth behind our wall, he looketh forth at the windows, shewing himself through the lattice" (Song 2:9).

The Lord stands outside the wall looking through the window. He waits patiently for us and calls out softly, "Rise up, my darling! Come away with me, my fair one!" Then He waits for our response. Will we agree to "come away?" Will we leave the distractions of the world and come away? Will we leave our normal routine and sit with Him awhile?

He shows Himself, letting us know He is there. He looks through the window slowly revealing His presence and hoping we will notice Him. Do we? We sit alone, content with the blessings He has provided, while the Lord of glory is alone and lonely. And, as hard as it is to believe, He longs for our company, for intimacy with us. He wants us to know we have a higher purpose. He yearns for us to go deeper, and bask in His presence, in His arms, where we can finally rest and find true contentment and security.

Our heavenly Bridegroom is not content that we merely hear stories about His manifest presence. He wants us to draw near and fellowship with Him in the secret place. He longs to bring us into the experiential reality of His manifest presence. It is there that He awakens the desire for more of Him and reveals the deeper things of the Spirit.

The word "manifest" means to make visible to one or more of our five senses. Within that sacred precinct are the very chambers where we enter His manifest presence. Because the Lord has been repeatedly wounded by those who take His presence carelessly, He is hesitant to openly make Himself known to them. Therefore, He cautiously approaches those He seeks (looking through the window) to discover whether we really desire Him or if it is mere lip service.

Do we relate to only His "omnipresence," that includes merely a sense of divine presence, but stops there without going further? The omnipresence is just a doorway leading us into His manifest presence where we meet Him as a person and have a personal visitation from a personal Christ.

I see You standing alone looking through the window. I will not keep You standing there. I bid You come and sit with me in sweet intimacy. Reveal Yourself to me, for I am not content with just hearing stories of Your presence. I want to discover You for myself!

Footsteps of the Flock

"Tell me, O thou whom my soul loveth, where thou feedest, where thou makest thy flock to rest at noon: for why should I be as one that turneth aside by the flocks of thy companions? If thou know not, O thou fairest among women, go thy way forth by the footsteps of the flock, and feed thy kids beside the shepherds' tents." (Song 1:7-8).

I often revisit the same vision when I pray. I see a long path leading far into the distance. The sun is just setting on the horizon. Lanterns light both sides of the path guiding the traveler toward his goal. These lanterns were carefully positioned one by one by pioneers from ages gone by, each lantern illuminating the way for the spiritually sensitive travelers who seek the secrets of the well-lit path.

God places a deep desire within His Bride to spend time with Him, to feed upon Him. She is encouraged by the testimony of others, but doesn't want to stop there. She must forge ahead herself.

She cries out with intense spiritual hunger, "Tell me more." She needs more than just the overflow of someone else's experience; *"The flock of thy companions"* is no longer enough. She needs more than just the testimony or ministry of another, which cannot address her deepest need. She began a diligent search for those who really know Him personally, those few who understand *His ways— not just His acts.*

She must follow the *"footsteps of the flock,"* journeying this road less traveled to learn their secrets and follow their example to the *"Shepherd's tent."* It is there she too, will be captivated by His love and favor. It is at the *Shepherd's tent* that she learns truths only discovered experientially, by getting to know the personal God who embraces her in a deeply personal way.

There the *pioneer* is transformed into the *light bearer,* and the journey now becomes a testimony borne of personal intimacy. Others receive hope as they follow the *"footsteps of the flock."* The path is illuminated by the precious truth of their testimony and soon becomes a guiding light, a beacon lighting the way for others who clearly sense God's approval on them as His fragrance flows from their lives.

A pillar of the faith placed each lantern on that long path that I saw in my vision. The lantern represents the testimonies of those who trod the *"footsteps of the flock"* before us. Precious ones like Walter Beuttler, Brother Lawrence, Hattie Hammond, and Praying Hyde. They left a lantern, a landmark (testimony) for the journey so we may more clearly see the path ahead. We have hope that we too may reach the *"Shepherd's tent,"* to know Him and receive a personal revelation from the One who loves us most.

As other pioneers of the past have blazed a trail led by Your presence, let me also blaze a trail and leave a legacy for others who come behind me.

The Word of the Lord

Then the LORD touched my mouth and said, "See, I have put my words in your mouth!" (Jer. 1: 9, NLT)

"Now go, and do as I have told you. I will help you speak well, and I will tell you what to say" (Ex. 4:12, NLT).

The Lord is searching for those who will carry His words. True disciples who will enshrine His vision—in their hearts. With a holy fire on their lips, they will speak forth His heart to a spiritually famished generation. Hungry lovers of God are desperate to hear **"the word of the Lord."** They want His heart to be communicated to them.

In the last days, there will be some who will prefer to "sermonize" rather than "wait on Him" for *"divine bread"* from heaven. It is far easier to pull a message off the internet or from a book than to seek earnestly for fresh manna. This is not to say that we can't learn from others, but when our messages lack substance and anointing because we did not seek *Him* first, God is saddened and we are shortchanged, without the true manna from heaven He wants to give us. He desires to fill our mouths with the thoughts of His heart for that particular moment in time. And when ministers cease to get real messages from God their sermons become empty and heartless.

Oh God, let my words be Your words! Please let me carry Your heart to a hungry, famished people that long for You and don't realize it yet. Let me not settle for mere sermons, but touch my lips with a coal of fire from Your altar that I may communicate Your deep heart cry from the throne room.

The Word of the Lord (2)

"They couldn't take their eyes off them—Peter and John standing there so confident, so sure of themselves! Their fascination deepened when they realized these two were laymen with no training in Scripture or formal education. They recognized them as companions of Jesus" (Acts 4:13, MSG).

One summer, I was vacationing in northern Michigan. The beauty and splendor were awesome, overlooking the lake, as I waited on Him. He gave me a message for the people of a particular congregation, and His manifest presence was so strong that I began to weep. The Lord gave me a vision of how I should minister and how specifically I should conduct the altar call. He told me to have everyone stand and ask the Lord how much He loved them. In my vision, I saw people asking the question, as the Spirit, like a wave of the ocean, came rolling into our midst. I saw people weeping and falling on their faces before God. The vision gripped my heart.

The day arrived for me to give my message. I had spent many days seeking Him and asking Him for "the word of the Lord." About halfway through my message, the Spirit came into the service. The Holy Spirit visibly touched the people. At the end of the message, I followed the Lord's directions exactly for the altar call. All at once, just as I had seen in my vision, the Spirit moved. I watched with amazement as my vision literally unfolded before me exactly as I had seen it. I was overcome with gratitude and excitement at the power of our wonderful Holy Spirit.

When we say what God wants us to say and do what He wants us to do, He will bless us with humble confidence, and this confidence will cause a *"fascination to deepen"* inside others. Though they won't understand why, many will be fed by His words flowing through us.

Lord, apart from You I am not a man of great ability or great wisdom. I fall short so often. I thank You that I can be with You and know You earnestly. This knowledge will compensate for my shortcomings. Give me a heart to know You in an even greater capacity. Let others perceive that I have been with You, that they may see my light and glorify You in heaven.

The Word of the Lord (3)

"**And my word and my preaching were not in persuasive words of human wisdom, but in demonstration of the Spirit and of power, that your faith may not be in the wisdom of men, but in the power of God**" (I Cor. 2:1-5, Young's Translation).

Those who are spiritually receptive will feel the *"Spirit and Life" of God* flowing into them, as a result of something apart from the content of the message, and they'll want more, as they recognize that their spirits are, for the very first time, actually being fed with the *"word of the Lord."* Others will also be inspired by the *"demonstration of the Spirit"* and power of Your message and be hungry to seek You for themselves.

God is seeking for willing servants, instruments through which He can convey His message to the people. His message will have a distinct sound almost like a "clapping of thunder." I have heard the sound many times throughout the years. There is a power, presence and an anointing distinct in the words of God's messenger that can only be spiritually discerned. This *clapping of thunder* is not a matter of sound volume, but can be heard by an inner ear tuned to the sound of the Spirit.

"The word of the Lord" will shake up Satan's kingdom and tear down religious strongholds. Bondages will break, and chains will fall. *"Spirit and Life"* will provide spiritual substance to the hungry and desperate.

Sermonizing or intellectual pursuits fueled by man's wisdom will never be an effective substitute for the transforming power of *"the word of the Lord."* He desires that we carry a message, a revelation, a communication from God, to be passed on to God's people at the prescribed moment. In fact, our precious Lord is looking for surrendered vessels to storm the heavens for the *"word of the Lord"* and not just open an encyclopedia before the people. It is essential that God's "vessels" know what it is to have an open heaven, a personal encounter, and a personal revelation of God.

"...the heavens were opened to me, and I saw visions of God...The LORD gave a message to me...and I felt the hand of the LORD take hold of me" (Ezek. 1:1-3, NLT).

Sermons will never do, dear Lord. I want an open heaven wherever I go. Let me know You with my heart, not just my head. Give me the word of the Lord, and may that hot coal of fire from Your altar be ablaze in my soul!

Spirit of Prophecy

Rev. 19:10

Let my words resound like the clapping of thunder
That Satan's kingdom be broken asunder.

Power and Presence, anointing my words
Cries in the wilderness, may they be heard.

"Spirituals" come from that other realm
The crucified life, with Christ at the helm.

I'm asking for the "tongue of the learned"
Obtained through communion, and not mere concern.

The "more excellent way" of "identification"
And not only casual supplication.

The "spirit of prophecy" is more than a gift
Sent from on high for spiritual "lift."

The Lord wakes me up "morning by morning"
And in the night season without any warning.

I "sup" with the Master and He with me
    I sit at His feet in His company.

My "inner ears" open that I may hear
The spirit of prophecy, distinct and clear.

That gift can be yours, but there is a price
    But oh, it's well worth any sacrifice.

----Steve Porter

Impartation

"I long to see you so that I may impart to you some spiritual gift to make you strong—"
(Rom. 1:11).

"I love them that love me; and those that seek me early shall find me. That I may cause those that love me to inherit substance; and I will fill their treasures"
(Prov. 8:17, 21).

Though they are similar and work hand in hand, there is a significant difference between an "anointing" and an ability to "impart." To be anointed means we have a special "divine grace" and "enabling" to do things. Under the anointing we are able to sing, preach, teach and minister more effectively. The ability to "impart" includes the anointing but is not limited in the same way. With the gift of impartation whatever we do or say under the anointing will deeply impact those who hear. Also, the very "substance" of Jesus' being will be imparted into the spirit of those who are hungry. When we speak, they will say, "I have been fed!" What they really are saying is "My spirit cfhas received impartation. Spirit and life, even the very DNA of God has filled my soul."

The ability to impart reflects the deep and ongoing intimate relationship we have with Jesus in His manifest presence (for those who seek Him early). This promise, "I will fill their treasures," is the direct result of impartation. A devoted believer who has the ability to impart will stand out from all others. As we soak in His manifest presence, we hear the heart of God and we speak what we hear under an anointing. The words then become spirit and life to those who hear, and create a deep hunger for more of God.

Jesus, in Your presence I receive "spirit and life" and am changed. I desire to impart spirit and life everywhere I go. I want to hear whispers from the throne room to impart to those who are hungry for more.

Amish Farmer

"For I know the plans I have for you," declares the LORD, "plans to prosper you and not to harm you, plans to give you hope and a future" (Jer. 29:11).

One of my greatest inspirations is my Grandpa Yost Byler. I have spent many hours thinking about him and the legacy he left me. Being Amish, he followed their "rigid guidelines" and "obstinate rules." Yet, he still struggled with alcohol and chain smoking. A dear Pentecostal Christian lady would sometimes stop at his home to share the message of God's love. Grandpa, who was trained otherwise, was mean to her and tried to ignore this lady at all costs. But her persistent visits made all the difference to my family.

The Amish were never in a hurry to leave their religion of rigid rules to become "Yankees" because if they ever left the Amish church they were "shunned" and estranged from everything they knew. One day this same lady returned and Grandpa's heart just melted; he was gloriously saved (born again). I wish I could have been there that day because I'm sure it was moving. He then left the Amish church forever.

Sometime later a traveling preacher came to town to hold tent meetings. Grandpa came and stood in the back wearing his new Mennonite clothes. His heart was deeply moved by the message. He knew he needed more than just a list of regulations. He needed a living relationship with a living Christ. I can just imagine him falling to his knees, crying out to God in tears. It was not something he was taught that changed him, but something he caught. There is a distinct difference. By the end of those meetings, God was preparing his heart for much more.

Grandpa attended his first full gospel service shortly afterward. He took his whole family with him to the service where an itinerant woman evangelist would minister that night. Though she was a complete stranger she picked him out of the service and hastened to tell him three things. First, the family dog had died on the road that day. Then she told him exactly what was in my grandmother's purse. Then she broke the news that my grandmother was pregnant and would have a girl. All three things were absolutely correct. Only God could have told her those secrets.

I personally believe that long before Grandpa planted the small church where he pastored until his death, his ministry was birthed in those tent meetings. He remained a close friend of that tent evangelist for the rest of his life. I so appreciate how he made the choice to follow God and "forsake it all," otherwise I might not be here right now. My mom would most likely have been raised Amish or Mennonite and may never have even met my dad.

Grandpa was known from that day on as a "man of great love," deeply moved with compassion for hurting people and for his remarkable love for God. It was said that whenever you went to visit him, he had his Bible on his lap. He was never seen without it. He read the Bible like a "love letter" from God, rather than a history textbook or work of fiction. He was also a man of great prayer and spent hours talking to his friend—Jesus. I never met him because he passed away before I was born, yet his life still inspires me. I know he's still watching and praying for his family.

So how will you and I go down in history? How will we be remembered? As people of great love? As people of prayer? As people hungry for His manifest presence? Will we be remembered as Enoch was, for walking with God? Create a legacy now! Leave your children and grandchildren more than just money and things. Leave them a spiritual inheritance that comes from hearing whispers from the throne room.

Dear Lord, You are writing the pages of my life with a stroke of Your hand. Let me be remembered as a man after Your own heart. May I die to the flesh and yield to the Spirit's leading in my life.

Life passes by
In the blink of an eye
And youth merges quickly with age.

"Teach me O Lord to number my days"
And fashion my life to your will and your ways
As I traverse this earth-bound stage.

----Steve Porter

To Sigh after God

"I want to know Christ…" (Phil. 3:10a).

To love God is to have fellowship with Him. It means to go to Him in prayer, to long for Him and to sigh with great passion. When we think about our God, do we smile? Do we sigh with great satisfaction? Does He fill our hearts with joy unspeakable?

If we really know Him, we will possess an overflowing love. Much like a young couple beams with adoration and tender affection toward each other, we also sigh and beam because we are so full of love.

He is my all in all. He alone satisfies the inner longing of my heart. He brings a smile to my face, a skip to my step, and a tender affection to my heart. He is my greatest joy, my never-ending peace, and my closest companion. He is my best friend, my greatest lover, and the one who keeps me company in the night.

How can I not sigh when I think about my Beloved? His face shines brightly in my soul, and His love overflows. His grace overwhelms me, and His mercies never-ending. Oh, what a mighty God we serve!

Oh, Father, my heart bursts with tender affection for You. I am overwhelmed by Your tender mercy and loving kindness. I will never again be satisfied with dead religion now that I've basked in Your intimate, living presence. I embrace fully the practice of that presence, no longer able to live without it.

Daddy's Girl

"I no longer call you servants, because a servant does not know his master's business. *Instead, I have called you friends,* for everything that I learned from my Father I have made known to you" (John 15:15).

When my daughter Alyssa was born, I was right there. I was completely awestruck watching her entrance into this world. I remember seeing her for the first time. I held her in my arms and cried like a baby as a love I have never experienced swept over me. Suddenly I knew I would gladly give my life up a thousand times to save hers. When our second daughter, Britney, arrived the same love swept over me. I held her in my arms, again overwhelmed by lovesickness only fathers can know.

Every night I would walk into their rooms and stand there, kissing their heads as I prayed over them while they slept. There is something so special about fathers and daughters. I wouldn't trade my girls for all the boys in the world! I took them on individual special dates (they weren't cheap either) and smothered them with affection. I wanted to train them to know how to one day choose a mate. To marry men who will love them as much as I do.

Consider our heavenly Father and how He must feel about us. He created each one of us special and unique, with fingerprints and DNA unlike anyone else's. Why? Because He didn't want "pushbutton robots" with programmed responses. He gave us "free will" to choose Him or not. He takes great delight in each one of us; He stands as an adoring Father weeping over us because He loves us so much. Every hair on our heads is numbered; He carefully remembers all our names and knows every detail of our lives. It is mind boggling how He can be everything to all of mankind. Yet, each of us has Him all to ourselves. Some things we will only understand in heaven.

Before we were born, He also pledged His life for ours 1000 times over. Because sin created a great chasm between God and mankind Jesus came to earth and died on the cross, willingly taking upon Himself the punishment for our sins and mistakes so we could go free. Now when we mess up as we all do, we repent, asking forgiveness and *God is faithful and just to forgive all our unrighteousness.*

When Jesus paid the price for our mistakes, He in essence took our bullet. God chooses to forget our sins and never remember them again once we ask forgiveness. The key is that we must ask. He won't force Himself on us because He is a "gentleman." Through the shed blood of Jesus, we now can have an intimate relationship with Him. In fact, God doesn't see our sins anymore; Scripture says they are removed as far as the East is from the West, to be remembered no more. He invites us to know Him personally, and not just follow a dead religion imposing an impossible list of rules. In a real relationship we yearn to please Him because we *love* Him.

Jesus, You call me FRIEND? Wow, it just amazes me that You would consider me Your friend. I do not want to be just "well informed" about You, but I want to "know You" as a close friend. Be my closest friend and the lover of my soul!

All Night Prayer

"At about that same time he climbed a mountain to pray, he (JESUS) was there all night in prayer before God. The next day he summoned his disciples; from them he selected twelve he designated as apostles" (Luke 6:12-13).

Oh...how refreshed we can feel when we spend a full night in persevering prayer. Remember the days when churches prayed all night? When talking to God was more valuable even than sleep? When it was more important than entertainment and the feeding of the flesh? There is something special about sitting with the Lord all night, and pouring out our hearts. There is something special about feasting on His presence until the dawn shines its early light.

Communication between you and God during the night can grip your heart and be absolutely life changing. "Melt my heart again with Your love, Lord!" In all night prayer we fast our sleep, comfort and rest, but we gain an increasing measure of the presence, power, and love for God.

When you seek Him all night, the nights may seem longer, but in the quietness of the seeking, you will find Him whom your soul desires.

When we spend all night in prayer, we declare a night of lovesick yearning for God. We are too consumed to sleep, choosing Him over our warm and cozy beds. Much like young lovers eat, sleep, and drink of love...The reality of God's amazing love overwhelms our senses. In making the choice to spend time with Him in all night prayer our passion for God is restored and our hunger for Him increases. "Things" lose their meaning and everything else grows strangely dim in the light of His glory and grace.

Close communion with the Lord can be accomplished—if we are willing to "pay the price" of sweet surrender, sweet embrace, sweet death of the flesh and the sweet embrace of His perfect will. Do you want to be the friend of God? Try setting aside a night of lovesick yearning for God. Watch your hunger for Him intensify, and His manifest presence increase in your life.

Dear Father, give me the grace to spend a full night in prayer before You! Let me be as my sweet Jesus who often prayed while it was still dark. Let me also spend quality time in Your presence. I love You,

Father, and I am lovesick for You. And while the night is young, I declare my heart is Yours. Take my sleep as a precious gift, for it belongs to You. Is it really a sacrifice, Lord, to bask in Your presence and feast at Your table?

Sin is a Mirage

"Fret not thyself because of evildoers, neither be thou envious against the workers of iniquity" (Ps. 37:1).

"If you love me, you will obey what I command" (John 14:15).

How can we possibly be envious of a worker of iniquity? Because the devil has deceived us to believe sin is enticing; it's like a mirage (hallucination) and at first glance, it seems so attractive. He whispers lies that urge us to just go out and drink like everybody else, then we'll be happy. Or if we just mute our conscience and go out and have several men or women in our lives instead of committing ourselves to one, then we'll be happy. If we just take drugs, snorting a little, smoking a little, shooting a little, we'll know joy we've never felt before.

Do we succumb to his wily falsehoods and become envious? Does it seem like Christians are missing out because of our adherence to laws in a book? Satan would have you think so. He hates God and those who seek after God. How cunningly deceptive that the "liar and father of lies" holds his enticements before us. The deceiver would have us believe we are bound up, restricted and hindered by the truth. And sadly, there are many who actually believe that we as Christians live miserable lives—because we don't drink, smoke, chew or hang around with those who do.

Yes, they think we're miserable—but in reality, it is God's truth that has set us free! We're full of the Holy Spirit; there is no high like the Most High. You can't lose with the stuff we use because there is nothing to equal receiving the presence of God inside us and playing a vital part in what Jesus is doing. He is the One who brings ultimate peace and a real sense of belonging.

But the devil continues to beset us with his mirages. In the desert, if you haven't had anything to drink in five days, you will suddenly see a mirage and think that the sand dunes are really big bodies of luscious blue water. So, you go and dive in, but the only thing you swallow is a mouthful of dry sand. You think you see a beautiful blue river surrounded by lush green plants, and when you're about to enter Satan's "Garden of Eden," you find nothing but wasteland there.

It's the same way with sin. Sin appears glittery and appealing. So, we give ear to the serpent and begin to envy those so-called "free thinkers." Urged on by his lie we reason, *I am restricted by all the laws in this Book, like they say!* But this precious Book (brought to us by those who were martyred for its perpetuation) is what protects us and enables us to prove that not only do we love God in word, but we love Him in deed. Is it a big chore to follow the laws and precepts of God? No! God has formulated those statutes to protect us, not to hurt or hinder us.

Regarding Moses, **"He chose to be mistreated along with the people of God rather than to enjoy the pleasures of sin for a short time"** (Heb. 11:15).

Lord, let me hate sin and love You more! Break my heart over the things that break Your heart.

The Beautifully Adorned Bride

One morning, as I was waiting on the Lord, I received a vision and saw the throne room. In the center of the room was a woman who knew the wedding was about to begin. She was anxious and glanced side-to-side, asking, "What am I going to wear?" Each time she said this, her face looked more desperate. On her back was written the word "Grace."

As her anxiety continued to mount, a beautiful Bride walked through the door. The "*beauty of the Lord*" was upon her, as her face was bright, glistening with the light of the glory of God. Her train was very long, shimmering with brilliant rays of light. Her countenance was difficult to gaze at, as the atmosphere of heaven surrounded her. On her back were written the words, "The righteous acts of the saints."

I continued to pray for some time, as the Lord embedded these Scriptures of Revelation 19:7-9 in my heart.

"Let us be glad and rejoice, and let us give honor to him. For the time has come for the wedding feast of the Lamb, and his bride has prepared herself. She has been given the finest of pure white linen to wear." (Fine linen represents the good deeds done by those who are overcomers). **And the angel said to me, "Write this: Blessed are those who are invited to the wedding feast of the Lamb." And he added, "These are the true words that come from God."** (Rev. 19:7-9, NLT). (Comments added)

We are living in the last days, when the Lord is calling us to walk through an "open door" into intimacy with Him. The heavenly Bridegroom is bidding His Bride to "*Come up here*" (Rev. 4:1), for deeper, more intimate fellowship. And there is but one requirement for admission: it is open to those who hunger for more of Him. And those who find themselves "in the Spirit" are being progressively changed into His image.

The very glory of God is being poured out upon those who heed this call to "come." In this "*throne room experience,*" the Bride is being changed from "glory to glory." Our heavenly Bridegroom desires that the atmosphere of heaven be poured out in our secret places of communion with Him.

As the Church Age transitions into the Kingdom Age the Body of Christ will be defined by two types of believers. Those who only content themselves with the permissive "*grace*," of their salvation and, in contrast, the diligent ones—having their eyes fixed on Jesus—who are preparing themselves like the wise virgins of Matthew 25 through their steadfast "*righteous acts.*" These "righteous acts "are not performed out of a sense of obligation, but rather are birthed out of a love relationship and deep desire to please Him.

The "*Laodicean spirit*" runs freely through the Church today and has slowly lulled many to sleep. Thus, they are not prepared. Our God has called us to "watch at His gate," and to "discern the times." This permeating spirit masks itself cleverly and convinces many that they are **"rich and increased in goods, and not in need of anything," when instead they are "wretched, miserable, poor, blind, and naked"** (Rev. 3:15-19).

Some churches today have replaced the "Anointed Word of the Lord" with motivational speeches. They have replaced godly elders with management teams and replaced God-appointed pastors, with hired Sunday pulpit showmen. They have become more crowd-sensitive than "Spirit-sensitive," relying on man's wisdom rather than the divine wisdom revealed.

Being "Spirit-led" has given way to a controlling religious structure that "denies the power." Bereft of God's transforming power, it substitutes only a shallow form of religion, dispensing a creature-developed mindset. They sing songs *about* the Lord, instead of becoming themselves "a new song." There is no spontaneous prophetic flow, no move of God.

These have substituted the tickling of the ears—misleading information and inadequate, inappropriate encouragement—for true divine revelation. The emphasis is on intellectualism (the rationale of reasoning), rather than purity of heart and mind—"doing" rather than "being."

In certain areas is found a mineral composite called *pyrite,* having a brass-colored metallic luster. These glittering deposits have lured many prospectors into believing they have struck it rich! Much to their chagrin, however, when their "find" has been duly examined, the assayer quickly determines it's worthless! The pyrite is better known by its familiar name, *"fool's gold."*

The devil is an expert counterfeiter, and he goes to church! Sadly (and with eternal consequences), gullible Christians, not rooted and grounded in the truth, will often fall prey to a "lookalike" gospel. Sounds good. Appears authentic. Easy to incorporate into their busy lives. It often passes for the real thing, but just like pyrite, its glitter is only on the surface. The Lord would have us seek deeper depths and higher heights—the real thing.

Laodicean Christian awake! Let your heart be stirred. Today is the hour of your *visitation.* Don't be enamored of the seemingly religious *"fool's gold"* that passes for spiritual nourishment. The risk of being left standing outside the wedding chamber with no oil in your lamp is too great!

As the spirit of Laodicea attempts to "blind" the eyes of the Body of Christ, Abba Father is busy preparing a Bride for His Son. The Bride is "buying gold tried by fire"—His divine nature. As we allow the "fire" to burn away our sin we are conformed into the image of His Son. His nature changes our nature so that others will say, **"Who is this that comes out of the wilderness, leaning on her lover?"** (Song 8:5)

The refining fire never "feels" good. But it's absolutely necessary if we are to be that mature

Bride of Christ. In the fire, His spirit reveals things we must shed so that His divine nature can be wrought within us, transforming us from "glory to glory." In this process we will embrace His kingdom and fulfill heavenly mandates. With our "invitation" in hand, we'll have our "garment" prepared (clothed with His glory), and not be made ashamed by our nakedness on the day of the marriage supper of the Lamb. (See Matt. 22:11-14.)

On that day, we'll not be frantically searching for something to wear, but rather, through our "faithful acts" of "supping with Him," and by answering His "*knocks*" on the door of our spirit, we will be "ready" and waiting—His stunningly adorned Bride.

"And they sang a new song, saying, You ... have made us to our God kings and priests: and we shall reign on the earth" (Rev. 5:9-10).

Lord, I want to be that mature Bride! I want to be prepared for that special day when we meet at the great marriage supper of the Lamb. I refuse to be lukewarm! May my heart never drift toward the things of the world; may it ever burn with passion for You!

Building a House of Devotion

"He appointed twelve—designating them apostles—that they might be *with him* and that he might *send them* out to preach" (Mark 3:14).

After I felt the Lord say, "Hermitage, PA," we moved to this small city in the northwest section of Pennsylvania. I had only visited here once briefly, a divine leading. I had been living out of state and on the day of our move I had a near-death experience and ended up in the ICU of the local hospital. My leg was broken in two places, and doctors placed a titanium rod inside it.

Upon my release I was unable to do anything for myself, which meant my wife had total responsibility for my care as I lay on my back during six months of intense leg pain. But it was the pain in my heart I felt would kill me. The previous five years had been tough. I faced many trials and sadly, even endured some intense attacks and wounds inflicted by the church. I was undergoing what some have called *the dark night of the soul.* By the time of the accident the stress had taken its toll on my health and the doctors weren't sure I'd pull through.

As you may have guessed I was a very broken man when I moved to Hermitage, PA. During that time, I decided to quit public ministry. Having nothing but time on my hands...I spent entire days in constant, concerted prayer. I had a small prayer room in my basement and spent eight to twelve hours a day for almost six months praying, fasting and seeking God. Little did I know Jesus would come to visit me there.

One evening as I sat in my special prayer chair locked away in that tiny room the manifest presence of Jesus was suddenly undeniable. I could not see Him in the natural, but it was clear that "His train filled the temple." His presence was so intense I fell to the floor. I held my chest as waves of glory swept over me! I had never before experienced such intense manifest presence. From that point on the Lord met me in my "soaking place," transforming me as I wept for hours, enveloped in His love.

I spent nearly a year hidden away with God. And during that time my prayer room became like a garden. While I lay in His presence through entire nights pouring out my affection to Him, God did a complete healing on both my emotions, and my health. Now I have almost perfect health and have been healed emotionally from my former trials and scars.

During the turmoil of that traumatic season of my life, the Lord taught me a priceless lesson. I learned it's not fancy titles, big ministries, or the applause of man that counts, but rather being a close, intimate friend of God. I came out of the fire...transformed. He became everything to me! He was all I had! I wanted Him more than any ministry. My love and devotion to Christ consumed me. I no longer sought ministry. I was totally content to just be with Him. I told the Lord I didn't care if I ever preached again, because being with Him was all I would ever need.

After a year in "the garden" the Lord spoke to me about preaching on the internet, so I started a weekly video program filmed in my little prayer room. I didn't even care if anyone watched...I only wanted to be obedient. The truth is I had to force myself to undertake ministry again because I was so content with my soaking place.

My little video preaching program grew and it wasn't long before I "gave it a name: "The Soaking Place." I had 5,500 friends on Myspace and 3,500 on Facebook, while many others watched on XP Media, Tangle, and Vimeo. I had no idea how many were watching. A large number of emails from around the world came in from those with broken lives who were touched through the program. Many testified of major encounters with the Holy Spirit while watching. I was blown away! I was totally amazed that God was using what began as a tiny internet ministry in a way that far exceeded my past effectiveness.

He has used me to minister to the hurting and broken, the shattered, even pastors wounded and depressed, those hurt by the church. He has healed the brokenhearted and restored what the "cankerworm" had stolen away. During that period, I taught myself video editing, and purchased a better camera and computer. The video program continues to grow, and I give all the glory to God.

For two years, I preached only over the internet until God began to open the door for me to preach elsewhere. At my first time back in the pulpit, I was nervous, wondering—would God come through for me? I was again amazed. It was like a bomb went off in that service! The Holy Spirit moved far beyond my wildest expectations! The move of the Spirit was so powerful that we had to extend what had been a short series of meetings to all summer! God was doing astonishing things! He used the tent revival to prepare me for more, reminding me of my call to the nations. Because of the definite leading of God, I was anxious to take the ministry of healing to the ends of the earth. I yearned to teach people about intimacy, the prophetic, and this incredible manifest presence of God.

Over a period of years God had brought South Africa to my mind, though I had no idea how His leading would work out. He had told me many years earlier that I would go there, yet I knew no one there and had no contacts. One night in prayer I was drawn to a website of a large ministry there. While on the site, God gave me a prophetic word for the pastor. I had to really put my faith out there to deliver it. The pastor emailed me back blown away by the word, which was timely and pinpoint-accurate regarding his situation. He was so stirred that he invited me to come and minister in South Africa.

That invitation, in turn, opened other influential doors for me. Only God could have pulled that off! The pastor was president and founder Dr. Jeff van Wyk, part of a network that included over 500 Bible schools and hundreds of churches. He and his wife, Pastor Marlene, were planting new bases of ministry in other nations and reaching the world through online classes as well.

South Africa's key leaders in the prophetic gave me spiritual keys to their nation. God placed me before hundreds of pastors who then invited me to preach in their churches. God was moving. All this led to an opportunity to be the international director of that network of Bible schools, Team Impact University. Since then, we opened a base here in the U.S., and are planting schools, churches, and bases all over the world.

I continue to visit South Africa and have been touched by the humility and manifest presence of God in the lives of these pastors, as well as an unexpected and enduring personal prophetic anointing. Many have laid hands on me, praying for the gift of impartation, and now my soul is aflame for God because of these dear South African ministers. Dr. Jeff and Pastor Marlene van Wyk and I remain the closest of friends as we continue to minister together and see God explode Team Impact University around the world.

We travel to South Africa and internationally, speaking in conferences, and each time the Lord displays His glory in the services I remember my little soaking room in Hermitage, PA., where it all started. Those two years I hid away in my prayer garden absolutely transformed my life. Long after the meetings are over, I return to my soaking place because this is where my heart is—the place where the Lord waits for me to come and sit with Him. Walter Beuttler said it best, "If you build God a house of devotion, He will build you a house of ministry."

Dear Father, I long to be alone with You in my prayer garden. I desire to soak in Your presence and be transformed by Your glory. I know if I'm faithful to build my relationship with You, You will use my life for Your glory.

Streams in the Desert

When my soul is parched and dry
When out of touch, He seems so far away.
I groan, I plead for Him to pour afresh
His satisfying waters from on High.

Listening for His voice, I come apart
And wait for Him "as deep calls unto deep"
And there my thirsting soul is filled
With rivers flowing from His very heart.

Begotten of the Father, Christ appears
In barren wilderness with healing oils.
With mercy streaming from His Father's House
And crimson cloths to wipe away my tears.

Fellow pilgrim in that desert place
The Master sets a table there for you
And bids you come and dine, your soul refresh.
Come feast on riches of His sovereign grace.

And though you feel you have no advocate
You're traveling on this road in solitude,
Unseen He walks beside, His presence sure,
For nothing from His love shall separate.

God's promises are true, and rest assured
That for the asking they may be obtained.
Know this—He'll never leave you all alone
His love is everlasting, like His Word!

----Steve Porter

"For I am persuaded, that neither death, nor life, nor angels, nor principalities, nor powers, nor things present, nor things to come, Nor height, nor depth, nor any other creature, shall be able to separate us from the love of God, which is in Christ Jesus our Lord" (Rom. 8: 38, 39).

Under the Apple Tree

"When you pray, don't babble on and on as people of other religions do. They think their prayers are answered only by repeating their words again and again. Don't be like them, because your Father knows exactly what you need even before you ask him!"
(Matt. 6:7, NLT)

One spring evening I walked to my backyard where I found a broken fence. I had never traveled beyond that fence in the short time we'd lived in the neighborhood. I sensed an inner "knocking" on my heart to pray. There has always been something special about walking with God in the "cool of the evening" as Adam and Eve did generations ago. I walked past the fence and across a field to an apple tree. The tree was in full bloom, its branches laden with beautiful and stunningly fragrant flowers. As I rested underneath the tree, enjoying the beauty of the season, I sensed the manifest presence of the Lord and knew He had something to say. The Holy Spirit began to teach me about "transparent prayer."

Every evening the Lord would meet me under that apple tree; I yearned to walk with God in the same way as godly trailblazers of the past. I desired to be like Noah, to be "just" and "perfect" for my generation. I knew that in order to accomplish this—to please God and gain His approval— I had to walk closely with Him. I didn't do it out of a sense of duty or obligation, but rather out of a heart on fire with a passion for intimacy.

Walking with Him requires transparency (unguarded, free of pretense) that only happens when we lay aside our agendas and choose to be open and genuine in prayer. Our Lord takes great delight even when we just share the simple details of our day. Beloved, He counts the hairs on our heads; how much more does He care for every other aspect of our lives? This kind of transparent prayer builds great anticipation to return to the secret place where you "sup with Him" and "He with you" (Rev. 3:20).

And as we come, note that He is not looking for fancy, complicated prayers.

The Lord desires us to walk with Him as close friends, sharing our hearts and "fellowshipping with Him in His sufferings." He desires that we open our hearts to Him and speak to Him "mouth to mouth" and "face to face." We do this by being real with Him and sharing our deepest secrets. We tell Him about our day and commune with Him, knowing He loves us dearly as we lean against Him, carefree, with our head resting on His shoulder.

The Lord will then begin to talk to us "plainly" and "intimately" and "without riddles" because we are "those after His own heart." Coming to Him without any hidden motive but to hold Him closely, will take you into deeper dimensions of the manifest presence. "Transparent prayer" unlocks the door to intimacy while making us pleasing to Him, allowing us to walk with Him, hand in hand.

Lord, as I walk with You I share the deepest longings of my heart. For You understand my ways and know my thoughts. I desire to please You with all my mind, heart, and soul. Speak to me mouth to mouth and face to face. For I desire only YOU!

Faithfulness

"But Martha was <u>distracted</u> by all the preparations that had to be made" Luke 10:40, NIV).

"But few things are needed—or indeed only one. Mary has chosen <u>what is better,</u> and it will <u>not</u> be taken away from her." (Luke 10:42, NIV)

Faithfulness is not just "outward" but is also "upward." What does it profit us if we do mighty exploits for God, but He is not our friend? We can keep ourselves very busy doing absolutely wonderful things for God, yet lack the power that comes through prayer. From that place, our works are not done through relationship with Him, but in our own strength. The Lord stands there all alone seeking "time" with us—because He has been replaced by other "loves." In essence, He has been neglected for the "love of ministry" rather than the "love of God."

When we do "things" for God but have not spent time in prayer, we have become a "hireling" rather than a companion. **Service for God must always originate out of our devotion to God. In fact, Jesus gently rebuked Martha for being "worried and distracted" by her many tasks and her resentment of Mary's choice. Jesus told her that she had lost her focus; she needed only one thing. That one thing being "intimacy."**

It is not hard to discern whether a congregation is a "Mary" church or a "Martha" church. The Church today must find balance. I have seen a great number of people get into trouble because they failed to embrace faithfulness as their upward call. They may be faithful and doing good things for God, yet lack the intimacy Christ really desires more than anything else. Because of the lack of devotion and intimacy they lack power and their spirit-man becomes very weak. Then when temptation comes knocking—disaster hits.

Churches that lack prayer and intimacy operate mainly in "performance mode." Sadly, they often lack the anointing. When the manifest presence of God is not in the services, what remains is "church as usual." This leaves people with a form of religion—but the power and accompanying life change is not evident.

I am convinced many Marthas have ended their ministries prematurely because they don't have the revelation of first things first—faithfulness in the upward call. We can convince ourselves all we want that we're doing great work for God, but if He's not our closest friend it profits us little.

We must be careful not to become like the "foolish virgins" of Matthew 25 who had no oil in their lamps because they were either sleeping or busy with "activity." Spend time today refilling your oil supply. You cannot "give" what you do not "have." I've heard many people put Mary and Martha on the same level, but we must be careful to take heed to the words of Jesus when He said *Mary has chosen <u>what is better</u> and it will not be taken away from her.*

Father, I thank You for a fresh touch from You today. I desire to put first things first in my life. Let my priorities be in the right order. I do not want to stand before You one day having done a lot of great things, yet be a "stranger" rather than a "lover." Help me to be zealous about keeping my lamp filled. I want to burn for You, Lord; therefore I will seek Your face and replenish my oil that it may spill over and touch the world!

Enoch's Walk

"Enoch walked with God; then he was no more, because God took him away" (Gen. 5:24, NIV).

I grew up in a little town called Madison, Ohio, a beach town on the shores of Lake Erie, located in the northeast corner of the state. I was fascinated by the beautiful sight of Canada across the lake. For years I spent hours, days and weeks at a time, making plans for a trip across the lake to Ontario. One day, when I was older, we made plans to actually see the other side. Unfortunately, while we were on the way my car broke down as I crossed the bridge into Canada, a huge disappointment. So, it wasn't until some years later that I finally made the long-awaited journey to the other side.

As Enoch walked with God in close intimate fellowship, speaking his full heart to his best friend Jesus, I realized that I too could take a walk with Jesus and speak to him as an intimate of God. I called these times "Enoch walks." I visualized Enoch embracing his kids and family, then picking up a stick as the sun was setting, and going to take a walk with God. I also picked up my stick and took long walks with the Lord every evening when the sun was just finding its resting place.

For years, I would take Enoch walks with God on the shores of Lake Erie. For those unfamiliar with the Great Lakes, it is best to see them as small oceans. You can't see the other side and would never venture across by boat. I'd raise my hand toward Canada and speak prophetic promises over the people. I would walk with God on the beach, weeping for that country, asking for revival. A deep sense of intercession would hit me on those many evenings as I walked. When I finally took the trip to the other side of the lake from my hometown, to cities called London, Saint Thomas, and Port Stanley, Ontario, I was overjoyed to finally see the people of Ontario I had so fervently prayed for, those many years.

My trip to Canada is something I will never forget. I knew God wanted to use me there, as I had spent hours dreaming of the Canadian way of life even as a boy. I knew there was some kind of divine connection. Because I come from a long line of Canadian fishermen in New Brunswick, Canada has always been special to me. Every year of my life, as I was growing up, we visited family in that area. My relatives come from a long line of French

Canadians and English Canadians on my dad's side. In fact, my grandfather was a Canadian, and my dad could have had dual citizenship.

Walking with God on the beach those many evenings reminded me of how Enoch would walk with the Lord. We please the heart of God when we take transparent walks with Him, sharing our dreams, hopes, and depths of our heart.

The Lord is searching for an Enoch relationship with people who will, like their predecessor, "walk with God." Enoch was nearing his fourth century of daily walks with Him, and the intimacy between the two was so rare that "God took him." Enoch had learned directly from Adam how to "walk with God" in sweet fellowship. As Enoch walked daily with the Lord even outside the Garden of Eden, he grew by leaps and bounds. Beloved, as we walk with Him in the "cool of the evening" we can't help but see our faith grow. "By faith Enoch was translated." It was something that he faithfully prayed for with complete transparency.

> Scripture tells us that it was *by faith* that Enoch was taken up to heaven without dying: "**...he disappeared because God took him.**" **For before he was taken up, he was** *known as a*

person who pleased God. **And it is impossible to please God without faith. Anyone who wants to come to him must believe that God exists and that he rewards those who sincerely seek Him"** (Heb. 11:5-6, NLT).

How could Enoch have faith when there wasn't any written Word during that time? After all, *"Faith comes by hearing, and hearing by the word of God"* (Rom. 10:17, NKJV).

It was during his walks *with* the **WORD** (see John 1:1) and his hours of transparent talks with our Lord that Enoch's faith grew by leaps and bounds. His intimacy gave him special approval and affirmation. It was said that *"He was pleasing to God."* God then rewarded his diligence. Enoch had walked so far up the "secret stairs" (Song of Solomon 2:14) that he could not turn back. He had captured the very heart of God and was found pleasing in His sight. We see a principle here: *Only by walking with God will we ever please Him.* Our God is yearning for someone to walk hand in hand with, and to speak His very heart to. As we comply, we will then be found pleasing to Him and receive His approval, being called "righteous" and receiving the privileged title of "Friend of God."

Even as Enoch walked with You and heard Your voice and therefore gained more faith, so will I, Lord, walk in deeper faith in You and take You at Your every word.

Simplicity

"Now there was leaning on Jesus' bosom one of his disciples, whom Jesus loved" (John 13:23).

When you go to God in prayer, do so with complete simplicity. Climb up on Father's lap and honestly share your whole heart. As a child leans up against his father and lays his head against Him, lean on your heavenly Father and rest.

If you love to soak in His presence and enjoy His company, tell Him so! Pour out your heart. He loves to be appreciated and desires to be wanted. I find it remarkable that we can move the heart of God, but we do. His heart is moved when we speak to Him with simple child-like transparency.

Why do so many feel they impress God with their complicated and fancy prayers? They love the sound of their own voices. They love to be heard among men, but God does not hear them. Vain repetitions and mindless babblings do nothing to move His heart.

Two men were both praying one day in the temple. One was a man of great intellect and stature who prayed in the company of important people. His words were eloquent and carefully chosen; men were greatly impressed by his articulate prayer. However, God was not, for the man's heart was far from Him and he only prayed from his head to be heard by men.

The other man praying was a man of no significance, no title, or influence. And as he prayed, tears freely rolled down his cheeks. His words flowed directly from the depths of his heart, speaking as though God was his closest friend. Others noticed that though he may have been poor and uneducated, he had been with Jesus!

That man's simple childlike transparency and familiarity moved the heart of God. It was as if a child sat weeping on His lap. His prayer echoed through the throne room of God, and with a gentle whisper the Father responded with great tenderness and affection.

O God, let my prayers be from my heart and not just from my head. Let my complete honesty and transparency touch Your heart today. As I climb upon Your lap in prayer, let me know you as a close friend. I yearn for this type of prayer life, not superficial prayers that only fall on deaf ears.

Valley of Decision

"If you love me, obey my commandments"
(John 14:15, NLT).

We say we love God, but do we really? Do we get caught up in the moment of our declarations, yet fall short when we face the test of true love? It's easy to make impressive speeches before God, but it's another thing entirely to remain loyal to Him in the valley of decision.

Have you noticed how the world is always pulling on us? Embracing the cross instead of yielding to the tug of the world demonstrates our love for God. We do this by dying to self and yielding to the Spirit. When we're tempted to yield to our own desires, we stop in our tracks and use this urge as an opportunity to obey His commandments. When we blow it, rather than sulk in self-pity and condemnation, we quickly run into His arms and ask Him for forgiveness. "He is faithful and just to forgive us of all of our sins and cleanse us from all unrighteousness." He then picks us up, wipes the dust off, and encourages us to keep running the race set before us.

To really love God means to do His will, to hate sin, and to embrace Him above all others. To really love God means He is number one in our lives, and we make Him our first priority.

Love is not self-serving or selfish. It does not think about what is best for itself, but exalts its beloved over everything else. Do we love God that much? Do we desire His will? Do we faithfully keep His Word?

Oh God, only by Your grace can we keep Your Word. Give us a heart to really love You. Let us not offer You long, insincere speeches. Let us prove our love for You by placing You first in the valley of decision.

Religion is a Dead-end Road

"Immediately they left *their* nets and followed Him. Immediately they left the boat and their father, and followed Him" (Matt. 4:20, 22, NKJV).

I respect those who believe differently than I do. I have many friends who are neither Christians, conservative, or even faith-based. And although I disagree with them, I respect their beliefs and will never revile them for being different. I've tried very hard not to be "self-righteous" or "preachy." This type of personality will not "make friends and influence people," but rather repels them from the cross they need to embrace.

If you are not a follower of Christ, please allow me a moment to share why I personally believe what I believe. I hope these thoughts will shed some light on the "why" and possibly help answer your religious questions.

Religion can be cruel. In fact, it was the religious people of Jesus' day who plotted His death. These so-called "holy men" obeyed every law in the Old Testament, but their hearts were so far from God, they actually crucified His Son.

You have probably seen the movie "The Passion of the Christ" produced and directed by Mel Gibson. The movie does a superb job of portraying the final hours of Jesus' life and how brutal the religious leaders really were. These men avidly followed a list of authoritarian rules, but had absolutely no relationship with their God. The gospel Jesus preached was packaged much differently than what they were comfortable with; so much so that they rejected Him as their "Messiah" and tortured Him to the point of death.

Jesus, who cared little about the rules and religious traditions of His day, hung out with tax collectors, prostitutes, and "party people." Then He called twelve of the most unqualified men imaginable to be His disciples. It amazes me that they all "immediately dropped" what they were doing to follow Him. What was it about this Jesus that made them forsake all within mere moments? They literally left it all to follow a stranger.

To this day Jesus offers something that religious leaders don't possess. He offers genuine relationship—love and intimacy, the ability to know and to be fully known and loved, that can be found nowhere else. When those disciples gazed into His eyes they were transformed and could never return to "dead religion." They could no longer settle for following so-called "holy men" who had hearts far from God; now that they had tasted the real thing, they demanded something authentic, something real, concrete, and tangible.

Religion today still preaches rigid guidelines and rules. It burdens me deeply when I see mean angry Christians yelling at non-believers and acting so self-righteous. PLEASE Lord, forgive us for that! I believe in "speaking the truth in love" but not in hostility and anger. Godly integrity is key. **When I "hit the streets" I want to take an authentic Jesus with me.** I've spent years hanging out in the parks, alleys, and even a bar on occasion to show people the love of Christ. Many have been won to Christianity as a result of it.

My good friend Joe Overfield has been by my side for many years, repeatedly proving his love and loyalty to me and to my family. He and I love going on adventures together. At one time we were both feeling a burden for the state of Wisconsin. We fasted and prayed for several days before loading up the car with tracts, books, and discipleship CDs. Then we headed down the Interstate toward unfamiliar territory. We prayed in the spirit and spoke life over our journey.

Along the way the Lord gave me a vision of a man sitting at a bar, depressed and alone. The Lord said, "Tell Joe to get off this exit." I told Joe to get off there, and the Lord went on to say turn left and then right. As He gave me specific directions, we followed them exactly and ended up at the bar I had seen in my spirit. We exited the car and walked inside, and immediately, I saw the man in my vision. We shared about the love of God and prayed for him. He seemed genuinely surprised that we would take the time to minister to him.

Afterward we continued on our journey, and our three-day trip was clearly anointed as we ministered to many strangers along the way, hugging and praying for people on the streets. That Sunday morning we were sitting in a church in Wisconsin when we received a prophetic word, that God was taking us on a journey and guiding our steps! We were blown away.

I was stunned by the incredible numbers of people that needed ministry. It would take hours to detail my experiences on the streets. I can remember pastoring in one city years ago and feeding and clothing 500 people in just one day. I still reminisce about hugging those people, holding the children, and hanging out with the ones the church had rejected. That was what Jesus did in His day.

How can I not drop everything to follow after You? For when I look into Your eyes I am changed. You far surpass the powerless form of dead religion; You are my all in all! Gaze my way again, Lord, and I will follow wherever You may lead.

Quest to know God

**"What is man, that thou art mindful of him?
And the son of man, that thou visitest him?"**
(Ps. 8:4)

I wish I could give you positive, scientific proof of the actual existence of our God, but the truth is I can't. **I do believe the very universe cries out there is a God.** Purest logic decrees that with a design there is always a designer. With a plan there is always a planner. My car didn't just materialize by accident. Someone worked hard to build it. This complex universe with its planets, suns, moons, animals, plants, and even our water all speak eloquently of a Creator, "You were no accident; your Maker created you for a reason."

Someone once said, "Give me an atheist for one hour and have him ponder how long eternity is, and He will finally come to the conclusion after that hour there must be a God."

What is our purpose for being here? Is it just to breathe and eat and indulge ourselves, perhaps hopefully do some good before we die? I believe we were purposely created for a special reason, to know Him as a close friend. It still amazes me that our God would even want to be near me.

I once heard an illustration that our understanding is like the size of a cup while God's understanding is as large as the ocean. How could a cup swallow the vastness of the seas? Many of the answers to our questions cannot be understood with our minds and can only be grasped by our hearts. It takes faith to believe. How do I have faith? I have faith because I have encountered Him many times as a friend.

I've had at least two dreams in which I have seen Jesus. The dreams seemed so real that I woke up in a sweat with my heart pounding. I was changed forever by those dreams when I looked into His eyes. Many times, I have heard Him speak to me and felt His comforting presence beside me. I have invested thousands of hours alone with Him in prayer over the years, and I could not have done so unless I was experiencing something life-changing. I have also seen evidence of the devil in hauntings, the paranormal, demonic activity, physical attacks, and have even seen him cast out of other people's lives.

During many of my travels to Africa and India I've seen things that would make your skin crawl. All this leads me to believe in a God who loves me—and a devouring devil who wants to destroy me. In fact, God has spared my life more than thirteen times, demonstrating His miraculous power. There was a time when I was floundering and even suicidal at one point, yet I heard His gentle whisper in my heart. I see Him currently making something beautiful out of the past messes I have created—a huge miracle indeed!

I take great joy and feel deep contentment in knowing Him in a personal way. Trusting Him with my life brings peace, and I am comforted to rest my soul in His hands when I die. The truth is you are not alone. He is always there. When you took your first step He was there. When you entered school, He was right beside you. When your heart was broken, and you were unsure you would pull through, He was there. He wept beside you every time you cried. In fact, the Bible says, "He keeps all our tears in a bottle." He loves you that much.

"You keep track of all my sorrows. You have collected all my tears in your bottle. You have recorded each one in your book" (Ps. 56:8, NLT).

In the silence of the night, He waits patiently for us, longing for us to just reach for Him. His eyes are full of "life-changing love." We'll have all the proof we ever need once we meet Him in a personal encounter. The chains of dead religion will never again shackle us; instead, we'll eagerly begin our journey toward personally knowing our God.

In this quest to know You I am changed and branded with Your love. This kind of intimacy must be caught and not taught.

Brokenness

Who is this coming up from the wilderness leaning on her beloved?
(Song of Solomon 8: 5, NIV)

Have you noticed that it was your pain that caused you to run after God? When we face disappointment, regret, and heartache we run into the arms of Jesus with the desperation in our hearts for only Him. The Lord uses the brokenness in our lives to draw us to Himself, even when we try to run far from Him. Why do we always try to avoid pain?

Often when our hearts are heavy, and we are crying out to Him with tears and we feel like we're all alone, this is when He is closest to us. God is attracted to brokenness. It is when we're weak that He makes us strong. When we're at the end of ourselves, when we cannot even take another step, when we cry a river of tears—it is then that He picks us up, comforts us and makes us whole. How can we be victorious if we are never a victor? How can we be triumphant if we never triumph? How can we be an overcomer if we never overcome anything? **So often it is through our heartache that we receive a revelation of His very nature, and we discover that He is the "Great I Am"!**

Freedom occurs when you truly embrace your pain and offer it to God with a broken heart. This births a complete dependence upon God Himself. Out of the darkness of your midnight hour, when your pain is taking your breath away, you can see how He has become the "wind beneath your wings" that lifts you into a higher realm of His presence.

Problems, difficulties and trouble come to us all. But we must learn to humble ourselves and embrace Him in spite of them. We must also be willing to embrace our pain and brokenness and pursue Him anyway. This will attract His presence in your life like never before! God works through the weakness of men. Don't allow the trials you face to hinder your pursuit of the manifest presence of God. Don't hide but rather seek His face and His grace. He'll give you a lasting revelation of his very nature so that you will cry out, "He is altogether lovely!"

Dear Lord I embrace You, I give You all my heart and my pain. I thank You for drawing close to me, for healing every place I hurt. Allow me to receive a lasting revelation of Your very nature as I embrace with trust Your integrity.

Tokens of His Communication

Unstop my ears to listen, Lord
To your sweet "still small voice."
In quietness of soul, I seek your face,
So grateful
For the treasures of your grace.
Master, you alone
Embody all perfection
And I in full surrender
Seek to be your mirror reflection.
All creation testifies of you.
In "speaking" tokens of your majesty
Open up my finite eyes to see
Your voice commands the gentle breeze
That stirs the rustlings of the trees.
Rising mountains, valleys lush and green
Flowing rivers in between,
They all convey
Each day
Divine communication,
Divine revelation.
I cherish, Lord, your presence manifested
And divine discernment granted there.
Current words
A current God

Invading the lifespan of a man
Making clear your master plan.
Like the sound of many waters
Your voice falls on my ear.
Come my Beloved One
You are so welcome here.

----Steve Porter

Mountain of the Lord

"The word that Isaiah the son of Amoz saw concerning Judah and Jerusalem. Now it shall come to pass in the latter days that the mountain of the LORD'S house shall be established on the top of the mountains, And shall be exalted above the hills; And all nations shall flow into it. Many people shall come and say, 'Come, let us go up to the mountain of the LORD, To the house of the God of Jacob; He will teach us His ways, And we shall walk in His paths.' For out of Zion shall go forth the law. And the word of the LORD from Jerusalem"

(Isa. 2:1-3).

My dad, along with my close friend Dr. Jeff Van Wyk and I, were headed up the side of Table Mountain on a hot African summer day. **Table Mountain** is a flat-topped mountain, a famous landmark overlooking Cape Town, South Africa, and is featured on the flag of Cape Town and other local government insignias. The main feature of Table Mountain is a level plateau approximately three kilometers (two miles) from side to side, surrounded by steep cliffs. The plateau, flanked by Devil's Peak to the east and by Lion's Head on the west, forms a dramatic backdrop to Cape Town and its Table Bay Harbor, and together with Signal Hill they form the natural amphitheater of the City Bowl. The highest point of the mountain is 1,084.6 meters (the equivalent of 3,558 ft.).

It is a noteworthy tourist attraction, with many visitors using the cableway or hiking to the top. The mountain forms part of the Table Mountain National Park. Since we were not up for the long hike, we took the cable car to the top. The Table Mountain Cableway takes passengers from the lower cable station on Tafelberg Road, about 302 m (990.81 feet) above sea level, to the plateau at the top of the mountain. The upper cable station offers spectacular views overlooking Cape Town, Table Bay and Robben Island to the north, and the Atlantic seaboard to the west and south. I was amazed at how quickly the cable car reached the peak. The picturesque scenery absolutely took my breath away.

<u>*Devil's Peak*</u> is a name that makes me uncomfortable. It just doesn't sit well with me. On the top of this mountain the Lord began to speak to my heart about Table Mountain and Cape Town.

, Table Mountain is Mine, and not the devil's. ...alous over it, because it is a monument of My faithfulness to Cape Town." Table Mountain is the mountain of the Lord! For it is a table set with a feast for Cape Town. Divine bread and revelation, the new wine of joy, fresh manna, fruit of the spirit, and divine meat from My Word are all set on the table, ready for hungry lovers of God to come and dine at the Master's table.

At a conference the same night in Cape Town I shared the vision the Lord had given me about a feast prepared for them on Table Mountain—the table of the Lord. We had a special visitation of the Spirit that night at the conference, and many were encouraged. I don't believe Cape Town will ever see Table Mountain in the same way again, for this special mountain is a monument to His promise that He will feed those who hunger for His presence.

God's presence is enough to drive you ever onward and upward into the mountain of the Lord. Even as Jesus went alone into the mountain to pray and meet with His Father we also should get alone in the mountain of the Lord and sit at His table to feast on His presence.

Once a soul has come to understand something of the indescribable joy of sitting in the majesty and holiness of God on His holy mountain, the question asked in Psalm 15:24 suddenly begins to weigh upon the heart: *"Who shall ascend the mountain of the LORD?"* That is, who can draw near to this living and holy God? Who can ascend to the summit of His dwelling place and gaze upon His beauty? What's more, who could ever *abide* with God in His house? The pure-hearted will see His beauty and feast at His table. They will rest with Him on His holy mountain and be transformed by His holiness and love.

> Behold! The mountain of the Lord
> In latter days shall rise
> On mountain tops above the hills,
> And draw the wondering eyes.
> To this the joyful nations round,
> All tribes and tongues, shall flow;
> Up to the hill of God, they'll say,
> And to His house we'll go.
>
> Michael Bruce (1746-1767)

I desire to gaze at Your beauty and sit at Your table. I will climb Your holy mountain and meet with You for divine fellowship. At Your table I will feast on spiritual food and rest with You. Up the hill I will climb and rest in Your dwelling place.

The Cathedral of my Soul (1)

"**...He leads me beside peaceful streams. He renews my strength...**" (Ps. 23:2b-3a, NLT).

There is a secret place where we can meet our God. The door is always open. This secret place is known as the **"cathedral of the soul."** Regardless of how busy the world is around you or how chaotic your surroundings, in this special place you can find refuge. You can be on a train, in a car, or even in a large auditorium full of people and still meet with the Lord within this great cathedral.

I take many international flights. When I fly to South Africa, taking the direct route takes over seventeen hours of flying time! Meeting with the Lord inside the "cathedral of my soul" helps those hours pass. While others are busy watching movies or playing games, I purposefully meet with my God!

Life's distractions can get you caught up in a whirlwind of activity. Mundane busywork can replace quiet rest with God. Noise can displace quietness, and the chattering of many voices can drown out the "still small voice."

Finding rest for our souls is not always easy. Often, we get caught up in our surroundings and the busyness of life. We often bounce from pillar to post, always seeking to fulfill the longing of our hearts with more activity. Always searching for the true rest, but never finding it in our daily routine.

Beware of spiritual barrenness that results when we fail to meet with the Lord on a daily basis. Our Lord desires to lead us "beside the still waters." These deep waters flow in the "cathedral of our soul."

Though all around us *"the waters roar and be troubled, though the mountains shake with its swelling,"* we can meet with our God and find rest. *"There is a river whose stream shall make glad the city of God."* There is a *"holy place of the tabernacle of the Most High,"* and *"God is in the midst of her, she shall not be moved."*

This special meeting with You is in the tabernacle of my soul where I "come and behold Your works, Lord." Where I can be "still and know that You are God."

The Cathedral of my Soul (2)

"Let all that I am wait quietly before God, for my hope is in him"
(Ps. 62: 5, NLT).

What is this great *"cathedral of my soul?"* How can we meet with God there? The cathedral is found inside us. We need to quiet our desires, and our racing minds, turning our attention away from outward things. God is waiting to meet us within. "Christ lives in me!" No matter where you are, Christ is waiting in the cathedral of *your* soul, longing for fellowship with you. Turn your thoughts toward Him! Let your love compel you to wait quietly before your God. Only by being quiet will we ever enter the cathedral of our souls.

The simple French monk known as Brother Lawrence (1620–1691) was determined to meet with his Lord within. Even while washing dishes, he learned to "practice the presence of God" in the cathedral of his soul. Therese of Lisieux (1873–1897), whose "little way" often echoed this same thought of being quiet before God. St. John of the cross (1542–1591), Francois Fenelon (1651–1715), and Madame Guyon (1648–1717) all practiced being quiet before God by meeting with Him within. A closer communion with God was a result of waiting quietly before God in the cathedral of their souls.

"Be still and know that He is [I am] *God"* (Ps. 46:10). Allow your love for God to be poured out before Him. Worship at His feet, and quiet your distracted soul, and meet your God. When I'm in a busy place I close my eyes (if I can), and I tell the Lord how much I love Him. I allow my heart to pour out before His throne. I then wait in silence for His loving response. I bask in His presence and worship Him. You can do this for many hours. Just being quiet, loving on Him, and pouring out your love before Him in that great cathedral of your soul.

Those around you may not be aware of your encounter with God, but that special meeting with God transforms you from the inside out. You can hear the whisper of God in the cathedral of your soul where His will is more easily discerned.

You, O God, are waiting for me right now to come into the secret place and meet with You in intimate communion. I will come!

Purify Me in Your Presence

"Purify me from my sins, and I will be clean; wash me, and I will be whiter than snow" (Ps. 51:7, NLT).

Wash me that I may be clean. *"Oh, wretched man that I am." "My heart is deceitfully wicked above all things."* Only You know this to be true. Search out all the things in my heart that displease You, precious Lord. Purge me from anything that offends You. Take it away, because it makes me sick, too!

Why do I hurt Your heart with my sin? How can I not see the pain I cause You? *"Create in me a clean heart;"* take not Your manifest presence from me. This is all I have, and life is not worth living without Your presence. Restore me, Lord, back to the place of innocence before You.

Oh God, you hold not my offense against me, You desire to forgive and you keep "no records of my wrongs." "Your mercy is new" every single day; Your grace is granted to me even when I do not understand how. Let my transgression cause me to deeply grieve as You do. Give me a holy hatred for my sin, and let me be consumed with only You.

Teach me your ways and help me obey You with all my heart. Direct me and tell me what to do; only then will I find delight. Turn my heart toward Your statutes and away from selfish gain and self-love. Turn my eyes away from worthless things and preserve me according to Your holy Word. Release the longing I have for You in my heart, purify me, and restore me.

May Your unfailing love be mine always; I put my hope in You alone. I will walk in freedom, for You are my deliverer. I delight in Your commands and love them. Give me a heart that is willing, that I may always return to You and away from foolish things. May I turn my heart toward You today and forever, that I may know You and worship You unhindered.

"The New Reformers"

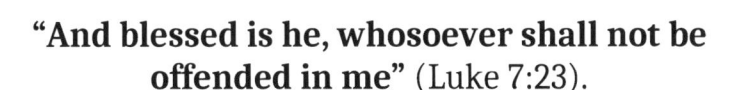

"And blessed is he, whosoever shall not be offended in me" (Luke 7:23).

And blessed (happy...and to be envied) is he who takes no offense in Me and who is not hurt or resentful or annoyed or repelled or made to stumble [whatever may occur] (Luke 7:23, AMP.)

There will be a blessing for anyone who doesn't reject the Lord because of what He does. We need to be careful that various mixtures of traditions, forms, legalism, rituals, and heathen philosophies don't replace the genuine move of the Spirit in our churches.

Otherwise, we'll suffer in some degree, the loss of the initial, anointed, mighty, miraculous, prophetic gospel. We dare not mix philosophy with the pure truth of God, thus diluting the gospel. These mixtures pollute the pure stream of water that flows. We need to remember, however, that the original flow of supernatural power and spiritual life can gradually wane, till the church is only left with a form of dead religion.

This process can begin as we become "offended" by the move of the Spirit and deny Him entrance. The Holy Spirit is a "gentleman" and will not force Himself on us. We can become annoyed or even repelled by His leadership and direction. Being led by the Spirit isn't always easy.

Nearly 1000 years of darkness known as the "Dark Ages" was a result of the mixture of religion and true faith tolerated in the church. The Spirit grew silent because His church became "offended in Him."

Since the Reformation, part of the original power and glory has been recovered. We are now in the season and time of the restoration of all the good that was lost.

> *"...whom heaven must receive until the times of restitution of all things, which God hath spoken by the mouth of all his holy prophets since the world began.*** (Acts 3:21)

The Church once again stands on the doorstep of reformation. **We are living in the last days.** He is setting up His kingdom and preparing the true

Bride to rule and reign with Him. His coming is imminent. We need Reformers to once again set His church back on track, to refuse "mixture" in the church—to pray the fire is once again kindled and that the smoke of His presence fills His temple.

Often the Church wants to do what is popular and accepted in order to be more responsive to a broader audience. In the interest of expansion however, are we losing our sensitivity to the Spirit in the process? When it comes to popularity, the Church has always missed it.

A.W. Tozer said it best:

"Popular Judaism slew the prophets and crucified Christ. Popular Christianity killed the Reformers, jailed the Quakers and drove John Wesley into the streets. When it comes to religion, the crowds are always wrong. At any time there are a few who see, and the rest are blinded. To stand by the truth of God against the current religious vogue is always unpopular and may be downright dangerous..."

In New Testament times the church moved with the mightiest power ever known on this earth. Nothing could stand in its way. In the last days His church will see that mighty power expressed as she avoids a diluting mixture, refusing to offend the One she loves most.

The crowds may not always applaud you on earth, but the larger crowds of heaven will always cheer you on.

God, will You use me as a reformer of truth? May I hand You my popularity as a special gift! For only what You say and think really matters. May I not fear the frowns of men on earth because in eternity I will receive the smiles of heaven.

The Angels that Gather (1)

"Do not forget to show hospitality to strangers, for by doing so some people have shown hospitality to angels without knowing it" (Heb. 13:1-2, NIV).

I have heard it said that you never know when the angels of the Lord will pay you a visit. A few years back in one of our services; I was preaching on "To Revel Under an Open Heaven." One of the results of an Open Heaven is **angelic activity along with heavenly encounters.**

We know Jacob slept with his head resting on a hard stone. While sleeping he had a dream of an open heaven. A ladder reaching from earth to heaven appeared and angels ascended and descended the ladder. When he woke, he called the place *Bethel* (House of God) and said it was the gateway to heaven. An open heaven invites angelic visitation.

One day when I was preaching, I had a heavenly encounter. This had never happened to me before. I was preaching on "Angels that Gather" when suddenly the Lord opened my spiritual senses and I was overwhelmed by the presence of angels gathering in our service. I could feel them everywhere! Through an inner vision I could see them everywhere in the room—*with my spiritual eyes.* I was awed at what I was seeing. This experience was completely new to me.

When I questioned the Lord about this, I was reminded of Paul Keith Davis telling of such an encounter:

"I was seeing both the natural and spiritual realms at the same time. Although my natural eyes were still seeing the people as they worshiped, my spiritual eyes were open to see the spirit realm. I clearly saw, with open eyes, angels standing from one corner of the building across the back to the other corner."

This experience has truly transformed my life. Though some may remain unconvinced, it really happened. An open heaven actually ushers angelic activity into your life. "God will give His angels charge over you!" Your dreams will become more than just dreams. They will become heavenly encounters and life-changing experiences under an open heaven.

Lord, I desire an open heaven in my life, in my city, and in my church!

The Angels that Gather (2)

"The Son of Man will send forth His angels, and they will gather out of His kingdom all stumbling blocks…" (Matt. 13:41, NASB).

On one occasion I was preaching at a conference in Cape Town, South Africa where the atmosphere was charged with the presence of God. People began to weep all over the auditorium when the power of the Holy Spirit began to fall. There was such a sweet spirit there that morning. After the service I was approached by a brother in Christ. He said he'd asked the Lord some serious questions the previous night, desperately needing answers. He was amazed at how, during the service I had stopped in the middle of my sermon and pointed him out, addressing each of those questions with a prophetic word. I told him I did not know his situation, but God did and gave him His answers. He spoke to me at great length about seeing huge angels on the stage as I was ministering. Others confirmed the presence of angels.

There is currently an atmosphere of expectancy for this generation to experience profound expressions of the power of God. We know of the promised visitation of the manifest presence of God to awaken the Church to her end-time Kingdom purposes. We are now beginning to see more evidence of this in the Western Church.

The Bible provides the testimony for an angelic encounter. The Scripture cautions us to

> **"Let love of the brethren continue. Do not neglect to show hospitality to strangers, for by this some have entertained angels without knowing it"** (Heb. 13:1-2, NIV).

The Bible records numerous stories of angelic appearances, indicating an imperative collaboration between heaven and earth. In the Book of Acts we read about the supernatural deliverance of Peter from jail. Paul Keith Davis commented on this subject, "Angelic appearances and supernatural signs awaken people from apathy and lethargy and reignite hearts that have grown cold or lukewarm to this reality."

During the early 20th Century, Maria Woodworth-Etter's ministry was set apart by amazing manifestations of spiritual signs and miraculous wonders much like those experienced by the early apostolic believers. A missionary to South Africa, John G. Lake was used powerfully as a healing evangelist all over America as well. History now documents wonderful miracles and spiritual wonders the Lord accomplished through this humble servant.

Caution: We don't seek after angels or signs and wonders, but only His precious Holy Spirit. Angels are servants of God and never to be worshiped. In these last days we must keep things in their proper biblical order. Ultimately, our highest purpose on earth is to delight in God and reflect the love of Jesus to a desperate and deprived generation. We simply cannot finish this mandate in our own strength. We need His empowering manifest presence and gathering angels to awaken the Church to her end-time Kingdom purposes.

Jesus, I am not seeking after a sign or a wonder, I am not seeking after an angel, but I do desire You and an open heaven. Let signs follow after me! Bring the atmosphere of heaven into my life today!

The Wilderness Way

I'll go where You lead me dear Lord, I said,
Not knowing what all that would mean,
Not knowing ahead was a wilderness,
Anguish, and trials unforeseen.

A place where the howling winds of fear
Would ravage my soul, spawning doubt,
Where painful and shattering memories
Would echo within and without.

Those smiling faces and double tongues
Rending my heart anew
Shriveled, I cower again, in this place
As they pass one by one in review.

Why am I here, Lord? I prayed as I cried
And He gently took my hand.
"To purge and prepare you" the Master said.
"Someday you will understand."

"For I too have walked in the wilderness
Tasting contempt and decline.
The "wilderness" precedes the "Promised Land."
And He mingled His tears with mine.

"With lessons you learn in the wilderness
Reclaim what the enemy stole.
Your destiny lies far beyond this place,
The Holiness Highway your goal."

"Whom the Lord loveth He chastens" betimes.
Our faith He does put to the test.
And that "night of the soul" makes us tender
As we seek His peace and sweet rest.

When the wilderness shadows were lifted
The sovereign Creator would fill
My heart and my life with His own design
For I'd crucified there *my* will!

----Steve Porter

Focus

God is our refuge and strength, an ever-present help in trouble. (Ps.46:1, NIV)

Christians are not exempt from storms. Waves of troubled waters often splash upon us. Afflictions are visited upon all of us. The familiar poem by Annie Johnson Flint reminds us:

> God has not promised skies always blue,
> Flower-strewn pathways all of life through.
> God has not promised sun without rain
> Joy without sorrow, peace without pain.

As Jesus lay sleeping in the boat, the storm came and filled the disciples with fear. They had the miracle-working Jesus in their boat, but they were focused on the storm and what might happen to them as a result of it.

In another incident, Jesus beckoned Peter to come to Him as He stood upon the waters. When Peter obeyed the Master's instructions he too walked upon the water. But when his concentration was diverted and he realized the "impossibility"of what he was doing—Peter began to sink. He focused on the choppy waters instead of the Lord.

The same is true of you and me today. Just as Peter began to sink into the perilous waters, we too will sink if we lose our focus and take our eyes off Jesus. Many of you reading this are facing storms of various kinds, as adverse circumstances swirl around you. Don't lose your focus! Keep your eyes on Jesus; keep Him the center of your life. As you look to Him, the gathering storms will not become an "undertow" to take you down. Instead, you will hear Him say to you, *"Peace be still."* And dear one, **you will not be shaken!**

Many of the saints are facing hopelessness and seemingly insurmountable troubles, as the turbulence of our times threatens to sink them. Where will our focus be? Will we stand our ground and cry out with Job: *Though He slay me, yet I will trust him!* Will we be unwavering as we hold to His promises, no matter what? History proves that our God is absolutely sovereign and **He** is the ruler of nations and kings.

That beloved poet continues with what the Lord *has* promised us in the midst of all our struggles:

What God has promised is strength for the day
   Rest for the labor, light for the way
   Grace for the trials, help from above
   Unfailing sympathy, undying love.

Don't focus, precious friend, on the troubled waters around you; refuse to be consumed by fear and worry! Rather, live your life according to what is written in the **Word of God**, and keep your eyes on Jesus. Put your complete trust in Him alone. As you do this, you will stand **on top** of those troubled waters. Right out there in the middle of all the confusion is the *Rock of Ages!* He is our firm foundation. Look to Him; He is reaching out His hand to you.

Psalms 46:
1 God is our refuge and strength,
   An ever-present help in trouble.
2 Therefore, we will not fear, though the earth give way
   And the mountains fall into the heart of the sea,
3 Though its waters roar and foam
   And the mountains quake with their surging.

Lord Jesus, We look to You for our safety and wellbeing. When the choppy seas of trouble, burdens and cares beyond bearing, rage and roar around us—keep us from debilitating fear. When we seem to lose our focus, draw our attention back to You. When it seems certain we're sinking, help us to take the hand You extend to us. Speak peace to our hearts and peace to our lives. Amen.

Comparing

"For we dare not make ourselves of the number, or compare ourselves with some that commend themselves. But they, measuring themselves by themselves, and comparing themselves among themselves, are not wise" (2 Cor. 10:12).

Do you compare yourself with other people? Do you find your value by using others as your measure? **The Bible** should be the only standard by which we measure ourselves, for several good reasons.

In the above Scripture, the Lord reveals that we are unwise if we're always comparing ourselves with others. To be honest, I don't want the Lord to someday say I've been a fool and missed the mark He planned for me! For that reason, I refuse to compare myself with others. I simply will not compete with others, and fall into that kind of sin.

Comparing ourselves to others will, without a doubt, lead us down one of two roads—**the road**

to pride or **the road to intimidation.** Let me explain hypothetically using myself as an example.

What if I were to look at another preacher and conclude: "This guy could really learn something from me. He just doesn't have my gift. His Bible teaching is just plain lacking." As you can see, I have just fallen victim to the hideous sin of pride, and wounded the heart of God, and in the process, turned off those around me. The Bible says pride comes before destruction (Prov. 16:18). This means it won't be long before God is no longer able to honor or use me to reveal His glory. Instead, He'll have to allow me to make a public fool of myself because I refused to obey Him and fell into pride.

We should guard our hearts. Many saints fall into the trap of pride when God begins to use them. They begin to *think of themselves more highly than they ought to think* (Rom. 12:3), and thus fall prey to pride and an unteachable spirit. We should examine our hearts and guard against that spirit each and every day.

On the other hand, I could look at another preacher and feel intimidated, saying to myself, "Wow, I could never have that kind of revelation and depth. Compared to him, I sound ridiculous. His ministry is so much more powerful than mine.

I don't know why I even try." If these are my thoughts, I have just fallen victim to the sin of intimidation, which is deeply rooted in fear. The Bible says God has not given us the spirit of fear! In reality, Satan is the author of fear and confusion, while the Lord wants us to have power and a sound mind that practices faith in Him alone. The truth is that living in paralyzing fear will actually reinforce the enemy's ability to hinder us at every opportunity.

When we compare ourselves to others through either pride or intimidation we open the door, giving the enemy an opportunity to operate in our lives. And let us not forget that when we stand before God we will give an account of whether we chose to walk in faith or surrendered to fear.

Comparing yourself with others is foolish, because God has created you to be one of a kind and wants you to be the best you can be by the power of the Holy Spirit. So, walk humbly and softly before God, preferring your brother above yourself. Pull the plug on comparison! Throw that false reasoning in the trash where it belongs, and allow the power of God to flow through your life as never before!

Lord of the Universe

I thank You for being a one-of-a-kind God who created one-of-a-kind children!
Keep always before my eyes the uniqueness with which You fashioned
each one of us. Help me to celebrate how fearfully and wonderfully I am made.
As I continue to develop my own personhood with excellence—being the very best I can be—help me to regard myself as a sacrificial offering unto to You
for Your glory. Thank you, my God, for giving me a "future and a hope."
Amen.

Climbing Higher (1)

"O my dove, that art in the clefts of the rock, in the secret *places* of the stairs, let me see thy countenance, let me hear thy voice; for sweet is thy voice, and thy countenance is comely" (Song 2:14).

Let us begin our journey toward His "chambers." The Lord has prepared stairs for those who hunger to climb higher into His presence. Our quest for intimacy can begin today as we seek the satisfaction we long for, and for which we were created. He stands bidding us to be partakers of His holy presence. He is calling those who want to move past the holy place through the veil into the "Holy of Holies." He is calling us upward toward personal intimacy and into a new realm of glory.

A deep longing is being birthed in the heart of His Bride for divine encounters of the God kind. Not just a self-serving desire for His hand, but an earnest seeking of His face alone. He is placing in us an intense spiritual hunger and desire for Him as He reveals the secret entrance to the stairway. It is there we can meet with Him alone. His Bride will not stop until she has His heart. These stairs contain greater levels of the atmosphere of heaven; they are a direct link between heaven and earth. With each step the level of intimacy increases. When we travel upward there's no turning back. We are transformed forever by His love.

I climb the stairs of intimacy one step at a time. I long to dwell with You in Your presence. I hear You calling me upward and I do not hesitate. Take me, dear Jesus—I am Yours. I abandon my old ways that do not please You and embrace You, my sweet Savior.

Climbing Higher (2)

"The king has brought me into his chambers"
(Song 1:4b, NASB).

Can we experience the same atmosphere as that in the throne room? Does God desire for His "manifest presence" to cover this earth? Yes! Yes! Yes! He is pouring out His Spirit upon the spiritually hungry and the spiritually discontented. He is calling us upward to the throne. (See Rev. 4.) He desires that we seek Him wholeheartedly. Many today are already ascending these stairs into a greater realm of intimacy.

Yet there are deeper dimensions in God (see John 14:2) we have not yet entered. Places in the spirit we still have not seen. These stairs lead into greater glory for those who desire the deeper realms of the spirit. They lead to His intimate chambers. The atmosphere of heaven is being granted to those who have fully committed to loving Him.

"I love them that love me. Those that search for me will surely find me" (Prov. 8:17, NLT).

It is in this place where divine mysteries are revealed, and Kingdom revelation is imparted into the lives of those who hunger for deeper levels of intimacy. God's secrets are whispered into the inner ears of His bride as she walks up the secret stairs with Him.

"But it was to us that God revealed these things by his Spirit. For his Spirit searches out everything and shows us God's deep secrets" (1 Cor. 2:10, NLT).

We're living in the end times, when God promised to pour out His Spirit on all flesh. Open heavens of His glory will be poured upon His Bride once again. The moving of His Spirit will refresh her. The Bride will receive her revival as she climbs higher. She will long for Him.

Reveal Your heart to me, dear One. I will get close enough to hear You whisper my name. I lean upon You and hear Your heart and am overwhelmed by Your tender love and mercy.

Climbing Higher (3)

"...and his Spirit searches out everything and shows us even God's deep secrets"

(1Cor. 2:10, NLT).

Entire groups of hungry "lovers of God" will experience *the "secret of the stairs."* The heavens open over their meetings, corporately moving them upward. As the church seeks intimacy first, signs and wonders, healings, miracles, and deliverances will take place. A deluge of His Spirit will be the outcome. How can anything stand tall when His majesty is revealed? When God opens the spout where the glory comes out, death will bow the knee to the King of kings. God is expanding the depth of glory in the lives of His people.

During this time God will do a fresh, new thing. Some will misunderstand; others will embrace this new thing. In the last days entire congregations will see healing. I see creative miracles happening as the cloud of His glory increases one step at a time. Demons will tremble, as the church is infused with the flames of His Spirit. Children will manifest creative arts and be entrusted with secrets from the throne room. That which has been shut up in the heavens will be released. Divine truth will be unsealed while the atmosphere of heaven will flow freely upon us.

Now is the time, and the hour is late, so prepare for *the Kingdom Age,* and get ready for deeper dimensions in God. The season is "now." The stairway is open, enabling us to climb higher into a new level of intimacy. "Stairs" provide a means of ascent toward Him, one level at a time. This stairway, and the secret entrance to it, is hidden from everyone, except to those who hunger for more. The stairs lead to His chambers and will become increasingly visible and accessible to those who desire His glory. He will reveal the way to those who seek first His kingdom and lean upon His breast as a friend to hear His whispers.

Thank you, Father, for You have illuminated the pathway to Your secret stairs. As I take my first step upward into the hidden corridors of the deeper realms of intimacy, You take my hand and gently guide me higher. Thank You for leading me and guiding me upward in my walk with You.

Sitting Before the Lord

She had a sister called Mary, who sat at the Lord's feet listening to what he said (Luke 10:39, NIV).

According to The Message:

"She had a sister, Mary, who sat before the Master, *hanging on every word he said*" (Luke 10:39, MSG).

In these last days God is desperate for a people who know what it means to "sit before Him." Only a chosen few really practice this regularly. In today's world we have many distractions that steal our time. But God is looking for those who will rise above the distractions.

If we're really going to sit before Him, we must cherish solitude and silence. We have to get away from the crowds, lay aside our schedules, and *"come away."*

If you've noticed, Jesus practiced withdrawing from the crowds to be alone with His Father. We too must discipline ourselves to withdraw and sit in anticipation before Him. In the process we will learn the "ways of God," as He imparts to us deeper knowledge of who He is.

In the silence we find His sweet embrace, His glorious face, and intimate communion.

"The secret [of the sweet, satisfying companionship] of the Lord have they who fear (revere and worship) Him, and He will show them His covenant and reveal to them its [deep, inner] meaning" (Ps. 25:14, AMP).

I like the translation from the French language even more:

"And *the intimate communion* of the Lord is with them that fear Him."

Friendship with God is reserved for the obedient. We must fear Him and tremble at His word. As we sit before Him to revere and worship Him, we receive the greatest gift given to mankind—"intimate communion" with the Lord, in the place where He can share His heart with us so that we become His spokesmen. In this place our hearts are connected to His.

We cannot be His representatives if we don't sit at His feet to listen. Friends do not share their secrets with everyone, but only with those they can trust. In the same way the "secrets of the Lord" come to those who sit before Him—those He can trust. Why? They take the time to listen. The spiritually hungry sit before Him daily hanging on every word He says. He speaks when we are alone with Him.

"There has never been another prophet in Israel like Moses, whom the LORD knew face to face" (Deut. 34:10, NLT).

"Inside the Tent of Meeting, the LORD would speak to Moses face to face, as one speaks to a friend. Afterward Moses would return to the camp, but the young man who assisted him, Joshua the son of Nun would remain behind in the Tent of Meeting" (Ex. 33:11, NLT).

Moses knew the Lord in a way very few others ever have. He knew how to withdraw and sit before him. Moses knew the "ways of God." He was a friend of God, a companion, an intimate of God. He also leaves us the challenge to get to know our God face to face. To walk toward the burning bush and cry out for "more glory."

Jesus cried out, "...that they may know You..."
(John 17:3, NKJV).

Do you really want to know your God? In the final analysis we must know Him. How can we interpret His ways to the world if we don't know Him intimately? He has been waiting "all night" for us, and He is still waiting, hoping, whispering, sighing. He wants to come in. He wants to be with us. What is our response? When He calls you, what is your initial reaction? Are you sensitive enough to recognize His knock from every other knock? Can you hear the sound of the Lord, found in His manifest presence? It is only through spending time with the Lord in personal, quiet solitude that anyone can be taught the "distinction in the sounds," and learn to know His ways.

Teach me to be sensitive to Your knocks. Let my response to You be right. Let me discern Your call and know Your voice from all other voices. Just listen to my heart beat... it beats for You.

Here Comes My Beloved

I see "light" glowing in the distance
Moving with Him as He comes,
My Beloved.
No other face compares to His
No other eyes can penetrate my soul
As closer now His hand outstretched
He speaks
"Love Me," He says in gentle tones,
"Love Me."
A mother and a father
All wise and nurturing
I am
And I will be to you
Everything you need.
And yet you fill your life with things and duties
Quite apart from Me.
Your sight is dimmed
Your hearing dulled.
I call to you
And hear no answering voice.
Remember when you lay before My throne
Our hearts entwined.
It's been awhile
Come dear one let us reconcile.

I'm missing you
I long for you to reach a higher place
And closer walk with Me.
My tears were falling freely
As He spoke truth,
My spirit wounded by His words.
Forgiving me He pulled me to His side
And warmed there by His love
I vowed to be
A dedicated lover of the Lord
Like Mary sitting enrapt at His feet
And hanging on to every word He said
I vowed anew to be to Him
What He became to me,
An everyday companion
Lover
Friend
For He, my precious Lord
Will ever be
My Beloved!

----Steve Porter

Tears at His feet

"And, behold, a woman in the city, which was a sinner, when she knew that Jesus sat at meat in the Pharisee's house, brought an alabaster box of ointment,
and stood at his feet behind him weeping, and began to wash his feet with tears, and did wipe them with the hairs of her head, and kissed his feet, and anointed them with the ointment (Luke 7:37-38).

Once when I was praying, I felt an overwhelming desire to kneel before Him. As I did so the Holy Spirit came and I became "unraveled." I could not stop weeping even though I tried. I just lay on the floor as His love and tenderness swept over me in waves. I was still for a long time, and just basked in His manifest presence. All at once in my spirit the Lord spoke, *"Steve, you are weeping at my feet."* I had the inner sense He was standing in front of me and I became keenly aware of weeping at His feet. This revelation kept me on the floor for many hours.

The warmth of His love was transforming me from the inside out, giving me a revelation that I would never forget. The man Christ Jesus came and received my tears as a beautiful offering.

Our Lord loves our tears. When we weep at His feet, we anoint Him with our love. To lie at His feet is to adore Him with our whole being. How can we not *be unraveled?*

Mary was always at His feet. She loved to love Him. She anointed Him with her tears, and our Lord loved her back. She got the attention of God, because of her deep devotion; she even went down in history as a great lover of God.

> **"She had a sister called Mary, *who sat at the Lord's feet* listening to what he said"** (Luke 10:39, NIV). (emphasis mine)

> **"When Mary reached the place where Jesus was and saw him, *she fell at his feet* and said, "Lord, if you had been here, my brother would not have died"** (John 11:32, NIV). (emphasis mine)

> **"Then Mary took about a pint of pure nard, an expensive perfume; *she poured it on Jesus' feet* and wiped his feet with her hair.**

And the house was filled with the fragrance of the perfume" (John 12:3, NIV). (emphasis mine)

Beloved Master, I long to lie at Your feet each day, to anoint them with my love! Every tear I shed You collect and consider priceless. Each moment I am being transformed into your image as I worship and adore You. Let my love for You grow each day. Lift me to higher realms of understanding. And Lord, as I seek to know You face to face, lead me to wider spheres of service. Purify my thoughts with the cleansing waters of Your Word. Search me and bring my will into subjection to Yours. Sweet Lover of my soul—guide me ever closer.

Fragrance

Jesus' anointing with oil by an unidentified woman is one of the most fascinating passages in the New Testament. Why does she choose to do it? The identity of this woman is mysterious, but some gospels identify her as Mary, the sister of Simon, which would make sense, if she was in his house. Where did she find a box of precious oil, and what was originally planned for it? As was tradition with the anointing of kings, Jesus was anointed with this costly and precious oil. Scholars believe the value of this oil (300 Denarii), would have been close to the yearly earnings of a well-paid manual worker. At first, it seems that Jesus' followers complained the oil had been wasted when it could have been sold to help the destitute, but in the end, they learned a very important lesson.

As was customary, she first poured the expensive perfume upon the head of Jesus (Mark 14:3), and the remainder she poured on His beloved feet. Notice that, in sharing the story, the Apostle John seems to have left out the anointing of the head of Jesus, so deeply was he impacted by the devotion he saw when she anointed His feet and wiped them with her hair. This is indeed a picture of love—devotion well worth noting.

Charles Taze Russell in his *Expanded Biblical Comments* said, "She took her hair, 'woman's chief ornament,' and devoted it to wiping the travel-stained feet of her Teacher; she devoted her best to that distasteful and dishonorable service. It was the strongest possible expression of her love and devotion. She gave her choicest treasures in the most self-debasing manner. She was bashful and retiring, and could not speak her feelings, and therefore she expressed them in this manner."

We learn that the whole house was filled with the fragrance; it apparently lingered there for a long time afterward. But even more valuable than the perfume was the sweet fragrance of Mary's incredible affection that so deeply touched Jesus' heart. Even today the sweet fragrance of her devotion still stirs and motivates us to follow her example.

There is an abiding fragrance on the lives of many of God's people. This fragrance of the Spirit does not come upon just anyone. It is costly and those who have it paid a dear price for it. The Lord desires to increase this fragrance in our lives. We acquire it by following Mary's example.

First, Mary bowed down before the Lord. This speaks of **sweet surrender**. As we surrender our all to God, our fragrance increases. Secondly, she used her hair. This speaks of **humility**. She was willing to trade her glory for His. Humility is key if we want His fragrance to flow from our lives. Third, she **sacrificed**, giving such a priceless gift.

The Lord spoke to me many years ago, **"Steve, the greater the sacrifice, the greater the anointing."** As we sacrifice for God, the fragrance of the Spirit increases in our ministries. And last but not least, Mary **soaked** in that fragrance. In fact, the perfume stayed on her hair and hands long after she left Jesus.

Through our costly sacrifices to God in devotion we demonstrate our deep, loving, and benevolent hearts, like that of Mary for God. As a result of that sacrifice a sweet fragrance is released from inside us, so that others will see that we resemble our Lord.

Master, as I am with You, release Your fragrance to linger upon me. Let it affect the world around us, and may others also run to Your feet and surrender all.

Even unto Death I will Love You...

"He will swallow up death forever. The Sovereign LORD will wipe away the tears from all faces; he will remove the disgrace of his people from all the earth. The LORD has spoken" (Isa. 25:8, NIV).

"There has never been another prophet like Moses, whom the Lord knew face to face" (Deut. 34:10, NLT)

Why have so many people throughout the ages been willing to sacrifice their lives for Him? Countless people have been burned at the stake, crucified, shot or hung, boiled alive, thrown to wild beasts and even buried alive. People would never submit their lives to such torture unless they absolutely had a genuine relationship with Him.

I remember hearing the story of a little Russian girl, carefully placed in a long line in her school. All the kids were told to say, "I don't believe in God," and then commanded to spit on the Bible. Every child in that school cursed God and spat on the

Bible. When it was her turn the little girl stood alone before the soldiers, wiped the spit off the Bible and then kissed it. She was shot in the head and killed. What was it in the heart of this little girl to make her willing to take a firm stand and die? I believe she joins the ranks of millions who genuinely know Christ through a deep, personal relationship and not as a mere religion.

Another example of a man who quite literally practiced loving his enemies during a time of persecution, and one for whom I have great respect, is Ignatius. He was a student of the Apostle John and a bishop of Antioch. He was put on trial in Rome and sentenced to be thrown to the wild beasts in A.D. 110. On the way to his death, he begged the Roman Christians not to procure his pardon because he longed to give up his life.

"May the wild beasts be eager to rush upon me. If they be unwilling, I compel them, come crowd of wild beasts, come tearing and mangling, wracking of bones and tearing of limbs; come cruel tortures of the devil, only let me attain unto Christ."

I know this statement is explicit, and it may shock you, but it shows us what a man totally sold out to God is capable of. I marvel at Ignatius' extraordinary love for Christ and courage in the face of such cruel torture and death.

In the second century A.D., when the Roman governor pleaded with Polycarp to deny Christ or be thrown to the wild animals, he responded, **"Bring on your beasts." When the governor decided to have him burned at the stake instead, Polycarp replied, "You try to frighten me with fire that burns for an hour, and yet forget the fire of Hell that never goes out."**

Polycarp was a mighty man among those in the army of martyrs. At the stake, he prayed that his death would be an acceptable sacrifice.

Martyrdom for Christ's namesake could well be ahead for the church. It's not polite to talk about this kind of martyrdom, but the fact of the matter is that as you become more like Jesus, you will probably be personally attacked, and your life may very well be threatened. America and other free nations may not experience the more extreme forms of persecution today, but we have no assurance of our comfort tomorrow.

"Remember the word that I said unto you, The servant is not greater than his lord. If they have persecuted me, they will also

persecute you; if they have kept my saying, they will keep yours also" (John 15:20).

Will you love Him unto death?

Father, I want to love You that way! Help me to love You even unto death if that's what You require of me. This is not easy and I need Your help and strength to even pray these words. Increase my tenderness for You and rid me of all faintheartedness.

Fellowship of His Sufferings

"That I might know him, and the power of his resurrection, and the fellowship of his sufferings; being made conformable to his death" (Phil. 3:10).

"Rejoice... inasmuch as ye are partakers of Christ's sufferings..." (I Peter 4:13).

One evening many years ago I was alone in my bedroom when all at once I was overcome realizing how self-centered my prayers had become. I had spent many hours casting my cares upon Jesus, and there is nothing wrong with that, for He bids us to come and has always been faithful to dry our tears and calm our worries. No matter the time of day or night, He stands there with His arms open wide, waiting to hear the deepest longings of our hearts. His loving touch brings peace and joy.

It brings great comfort and gladness that we have someone to turn to when the world turns its back on us. However, on that summer evening in the early 90's I knew I had missed a great opportunity.

I thought to myself, *When was the last time I asked Jesus what was on His heart?* Fellowship is the union of friends sharing similar interests or problems. To suffer is to feel the pain or distress of another. Could I ask my Lord what breaks His heart? Why not try?

I whispered, "What's on your heart tonight, Jesus? What burdens You most? Let me feel what You feel..." All at once I was overcome with a tremendous burden. I began to weep uncontrollably as the Lord said, "Child abuse hurts my heart, child porn hurts me, and abortion hurts me so...." Suddenly my heart was deeply burdened, and the spirit of intercession took control of me. I wrestled in prayer and I travailed for more than two hours. Sobbing, I lay on the floor until all at once this burden lifted and I felt joy unspeakable and full of glory.

I instantly knew I prayed clear through a burden that was heavy on the Lord's heart. Paul yearned to share the pain and distress Christ experienced. As we make ourselves available to fellowship with the Lord in His sufferings, our hearts will be consumed with what is on the Lord's heart. Our own self-centeredness in prayer has left us with little or no time to contemplate Christ's sufferings, let alone share in them. Sadly, the Lord has few trusted friends with whom He can share His burdens.

Will we stop talking long enough to hear the heart of our Father? I'm sure no man can fully understand all His sufferings, and certainly our feeble attempts are very limited, but God takes great delight in those who care enough to ask Him, "How are You doing? What is on Your heart right now?"

My prayer life has been changed since I started asking the Lord what was on His heart. I still take time to bring my needs and worries to God, but I also stop and ask Him what is on His heart. Many people never ask Him that question, but those who do bring great delight and comfort to the Lord. Will we choose to be still long enough to hear whispers from His throne room?

I can be so self-centered, Lord. Help me to take the time to know Your heart, so You can trust me to fellowship with You in Your sufferings. I will pray until the burden lifts, and see breakthrough come. I thank You that You can use my intercession to change history. What is on Your heart even now? Share with me Your burdens...

Chambers of Prayer

"The prayer of a righteous man is powerful and effective" (James 5:16, NIV).

Many Christians haven't taken time or made the effort to develop a healthy, vibrant prayer life. They see themselves much like John Donne, who stated,

"I throw myself down in my chamber, and I call in, and invite God, and His angels thither, and when they are there, I neglect God and His angels, for the noise of a fly, for the rattling of a coach, for the whining of a door."

A minister told of his Sunday school teacher, who despaired of his class and asked to be released. The superintendent persuaded him to try again, and to promise that every day for three months he would pray in secret, for every boy. As a result, every boy in the class was saved, and four of them became ministers, men of great usefulness and power.

A contagious, godly infection is "caught" when soaking in His presence, when our prayer closet becomes the womb of a watchman. When an individual develops intimacy with God, he inevitably becomes infected with His life and love. Just as infections spread when one person breathes on another, so God's breath conveys the same life-giving power today as it did on the day when He created Adam from dust.

It is through intimacy with God that we become infectious carriers of His life-breath. And a contagious Christian is an effective one. Instead of becoming overwhelmed by struggle, we should become carriers of His life-breath. A prayer room is a therapeutic place where we breathe in God's life-giving power. Prayer is as medicine to our soul. Do you want to find God? Then seek Him with all your heart! Wrestling prayer prevails. The fervent, effectual prayer of the righteous is a formidable and constructive force against the powers of darkness.

We mature through the desire He has placed in us to know Him. And we become increasingly like the people with whom we spend great amounts of time. The same is true regarding time spent with Jesus, as day by day, we conform to His image and even reflect His glory.

Father, let me develop a healthy and vibrant prayer life. I want to be a watchman—watching at Your gates and knowing what is on Your heart. Infect me today with the desire to pray, and infuse me with Your life and love.

Contagious Prayer

"Lord, teach us to pray" (Luke 11:1).

What was it about the prayer life of Jesus that caused the disciples to exclaim, "Teach us to pray"? What did they overhear in that special prayer place with the Lord? It was probably the most intimate prayer session they ever had the privilege to overhear. Their hearts were moved to ask Him to teach them to pray the way He did. Jesus responded with "The Lord's Prayer."

What would people say if they were to listen at the door of your prayer closet? Would their hearts be so moved they would desire to pray like you? Would your prayer be contagious? Only through intimate prayer, where we bare our souls before the Lord in transparency, will we ever become contagious. Of course, our goal is not to pray to be heard by man, but if they were granted access to our secret prayer closet, would they be moved?

Our prayer life was never meant to be dry, boring, repetitious and mundane, but heart-felt, devoted, transparent, and genuine. It's important to note that apathy in our prayers can result from praying with our minds rather than our hearts. Never let your prayers be mere words spoken from the intellect; rather let your heart cry out to God in simple devotion. Baptize your prayers with your tears, for they move the heart of God.

Even in corporate prayer meetings, supplication from the intellect is dry, dead and boring, but when the church prays with passion from the heart, this moves both heaven and earth.

Lord, my prayer life was never meant to be dry, boring, repetitious and mundane, but heartfelt, devoted, transparent, and genuine. May my prayers today come alive through the fire of Your love!

Desperate Prayer 1

"Likewise the Spirit also helpeth our infirmities: for we know not what we should pray for as we ought: but the Spirit itself maketh intercession for us with groanings which cannot be uttered" (Rom. 8:26).

We must respond immediately when this burden for intercession overtakes us. There is a price to pay for being an intercessor; it interrupts time for personal desires. I can say, "I'll pray now," or, "I will wait and pray later." But I cannot keep a promise to intercede either now or later. I can only say, "I will respond, if I am moved by the Holy Spirit to intercede."

A desperate situation requires immediate, desperate prayer. Half-hearted prayers will not suffice.

"The Disciples were not losing time when they sat down beside their Master and held quiet converse with Him under the olives of Bethany or by the shores of Galilee. Those were their school hours; those were their feeding times. The healthiest

Christian, the one who is best fitted for Godly living and Godly labors, is the person who feeds most on Christ."—Theodore Ledyard Cuyler (1822-1909), a Presbyterian minister and religious writer in the United States.

Lord, I will respond, if I am moved by the Holy Spirit to intercede. I will not put You off, or ignore You. You are waiting for me and I am here...

Desperate Prayer 2

"But thou, when thou prayest, enter into thy closet, and when thou hast shut thy door, pray to thy Father which is in secret; and thy Father which seeth in secret shall reward thee openly" (Matt.6:6).

"To the Christian who is not abiding wholly in Jesus, the difficulties connected with prayer are often so great as to rob him of the comfort and the strength it could bring."
–Andrew Murray

Signing up for the monastic life meant saying goodbye forever to a full night's sleep. In years past many have realized the vital importance of personal prayer. As I read that precious book by Andrew Murray, *With Christ in the School of Prayer,* and the book *Praying Hyde, Apostle of Prayer: The Life Story of John Hyde,* by E. G. Carre, I saw examples of those who actually lived with Christ in the School of Prayer, and the stories of these men gave me inspiration and a deep longing to be a pupil at this school. In spite of struggle, these men lived in prayer and fasting. They found solitude under His wings. I hope that their lives will lead many others to become the "companions" of our great High Priest. He wants close "companions," "fellows," and "partakers" to enter with Him into the sanctuary as intercessors. The High Priest of old had to enter into the Holy of Holies alone, but our High Priest begs for partners. This is what Hyde and Murray really were, and it is strange that we should be so reluctant to take up the great privilege of being fellow-intercessors with Him.

Daniel Nash began his ministry as a preacher in upstate New York. He saw revival twice in his pastorate, and then was a key figure in one of the greatest revivals in the history of the United States. In many ways he was to the U.S. what Praying Hyde was to India. He is known almost exclusively for his powerful prayer ministry.

When he turned forty-eight, he decided to give himself totally to prayer for Charles Finney's evangelistic meetings. Father Nash would come quietly into towns weeks in advance of a meeting, gather three or four other like-minded Christians with him and in a rented room they would start praying and bringing heaven near. It is reported that in one town all he could find was a dank, dark cellar, but that place was soon illuminated with holy light as he made it the place of intercession. Finney made this statement:

When I got to town to start a revival a lady contacted me who ran a boarding house. She said, "Brother Finney, do you know a Father Nash? He and two other men have been at my boarding house for the last three days, but they haven't eaten a bite of food. I opened the door and peeped in at them because I could hear them groaning, and I saw them down on their faces. They have been this way for three days, lying prostrate on the floor and groaning. I thought something awful must have happened to them. I was afraid to go in and I didn't know what to do. Would you please come see about them?"

"No, it isn't necessary," I replied. "They just have a spirit of travail in prayer."

Someone asked Finney what kind of man this Father Nash was. "We never see him," they said. "He doesn't enter into any of the meetings." Finney replied, "Like anybody who does a lot of praying, Father Nash is a very quiet person. Show me a person who is always talking and I'll show you a Christian who never does much praying."

In the book, *"Daniel Nash: Prevailing Prince of Prayer"* author J. Paul Reno states:

Though he prayed in private, yet he often prayed with such fervency that others became aware of his praying. This was not intended, but simply was the release of a deeply burdened soul. The lady at the boarding house became aware of his groans as he prayed. His enemies claimed "that it was impossible for him to pray in secret since, whether he went into his closet or the woods, he prayed with such vehemence that he could be heard half a mile away." While this was likely an exaggeration of his normal practice, there is a record of a single occurrence of note:

"In the revival at Gouverneur (in which the great majority of the inhabitants, Finney believed, were converted), Nash rose very early and went into a woods to pray. "It was one of those clear mornings," said Finney, "on which it is possible to hear sounds at a great distance." Three-quarters of a mile away lived an unconverted man who was suddenly arrested by hearing the voice of prayer. He could distinguish that it was Nash's voice, and this brought to him such a sense of the reality of religion as he had never before experienced; he experienced no relief until he found it in Christ."

You are no respecter of persons... What You have done in the heart of Praying Hyde, Andrew Murray, and Father Nash You can do in me! Give me a heart to pray! Let me spend time hearing whispers from Your throne room.

He Knows My Name!

"And the LORD said unto Moses, I will do this thing also that thou hast spoken: for thou hast found grace in my sight, and I know thee by name" (Ex. 33:17).

When I first began in the ministry, I was so hungry to see God move in my life that I truly wanted to hear His voice. Since I was born in a pastor's home, it was not unusual to see my parents have major encounters with God. My father could literally hear the voice of God speaking to him. It also seemed as if my mother had a direct line to God. Whenever I did something wrong, God would always tell her. It seemed like I couldn't get away with anything; my mother always knew because God would tell her.

I wanted that same kind of relationship my parents had with God when they lived the Word in front of me. They didn't just preach one thing from a pulpit and live another way at home. On Saturday nights I would drive by the church and the light would be on in my dad's office, where he was seeking God. The next Sunday it seemed as if

God had given him notes of what to say during his message because it hit so many different people in such a personal way. They were blessed because my father seemed to be speaking about what they were going through when they hadn't even told him about it.

I accepted without question the fact that God spoke to my father. He also spoke to my mother, a great woman of prayer. Whenever I think of her, I picture her kneeling beside her bed, praying for hours at a time. In fact, I remember walking into her room one day, picking up her Bible, which was completely worn out, and seeing the tear stains that had dried on its pages. I knew that if God could speak to my parents in that way, there was no reason why He couldn't speak to me in the same way.

To think You know my name! To think You would even want to speak to me as a close friend! You amaze me, oh God!

He Knows My Name! (2)

"I will climb up to my watchtower and stand at my guard post. There I will wait to see what the LORD says..." (Hab. 2:1, NLT).

I went into prayer a desperate man, fully aware that it was possible to hear God's voice. I had not been raised to separate the spiritual from the physical realms. God was very real to me, not just a fairy tale or some grown-up version of Let's Pretend. I prayed for about an hour and yet nothing happened; I didn't feel a single goose bump. I didn't feel anything at all. It was as if the heavens were brass and God was ignoring me. I prayed for another hour, and still nothing happened.

I prayed constantly for three hours and still nothing happened. After about three and a half hours, I couldn't help thinking I should just give up—God wasn't going to speak to me. But something deep inside me compelled me to stay in His presence. I knew I had to keep going, I had to have the same tenacity as Jacob when he wrestled with that angel.

After about four hours on my knees in that little church, God's presence entered the room and I began to weep uncontrollably. The wind of God literally blew through the church! When He spoke, it wasn't an audible voice, but it might as well have been because it was so loud in my spirit that there was no question that it was His voice and not something I dreamed up. I will never forget what He said:

"Steve, I am the God of Abraham, Isaac, and Jacob, and I am the God of Steve Porter too."

I wept for over an hour after that as I lingered in His presence, because God actually knew my name. I was special to Him. Nobody outside of my small community may have known my name, but the Creator of heaven and Earth did. After all the pain of humiliation and rejection I had endured from my enemies all those years, God knew me by name. My friend, He knows your name too!

Lord, if I have to wait all night, I will wait to hear the sound of Your voice. I will linger in Your presence and listen for Your whisper, I give You my ears! Speak—Your servant is listening.

Why Can't We Be Quiet?

"Be still, and know that I am God!" (Ps. 46:10, NLT)

We live in a noisy world, don't we? Everywhere we go, we hear people and things making noise. Some people actually enjoy the noise, and as soon as it gets quiet, they turn on the TV. When they're in the car they turn on the radio or a CD. Why are we afraid of the quiet? Are we afraid we'll have time to think about things that trouble us?

I would probably be considered a loner. I cherish the quiet! The 18th century is generally known as the Quietist Period in Quaker history. Quietism, which is not unique to Quakerism but which had widespread influence among both Catholics and Protestants at the time, emphasized the quieting of creaturely activities so that in the "silence of all flesh," God could be heard. I believe the Lord draws near to such a soul, and communicates inwardly to it. He fills it with Himself because it is empty; clothes it with His light and love, because it is naked; lifts it up, because it is low; and unites it with Himself.

I love to be quiet! To sit in complete aloneness with God, to ponder how beautiful His face is—to allow the stress of life to blow away and His presence to fill my desperate soul. To sit by the water and ponder the mysteries of life, and to speak to Jesus as a close friend.

We will never hear God if we can't be quiet and embrace the tranquility found in aloneness. We are really not alone, only separated from the things of the world to be that listening companion of our dearest and closest friend—Jesus.

Do we really need to talk on our cell phones all the time, play with our gadgets, submerging ourselves in the busyness of life, or can we take a break from it all and finally be quiet so God can speak and we can hear?

Lord, I want to hear You! Help me be quiet and embrace the tranquility found in aloneness with You. Silence the noise of the world and let me tune into Your whispers!

Dew of the Night

"Open to me, my darling, my treasure, my lovely dove, my perfect one. My head is drenched with dew, my hair with the dampness of the night" (Song 5:2b, NLT).

As I wrote in an earlier reflection, His head can become wet with the dew of the night when we don't get up to let Him get out of the night air and into our homes. This is a beautiful prophetic picture of our heavenly bridegroom coming to us for intimacy. He announces His coming with His presence. He knocks on our door at night, longing to be with us. His head is soaked with the dampness of the cool night air. Why is His hair wet? Perhaps, ours is not the first house he visited that night. He knocks at each door, longing to enter for intimate communion, but is instead met with rejection and excuses. As he wipes the tears away, He moves on to the next house hoping for obedience, all the while gathering more dew on His head.

He is longing to enter our homes; He wants to find a quiet place to rest. He desires someone to keep

Him company in the night. Will you be that person? Can He count on you to meet Him anytime He calls? It is easy to meet with Him in the day, but only His choicest servants meet with Him in the night. The sacrifice is a small price to pay for His companionship. How much value do we place on our meetings with Him? Would we rather encounter Him than breathe the air? When we value Him more than costly treasures His presence will be ours to enjoy.

Lord, I refuse to allow Your head to be covered with dew from the night. I will meet You in our secret place. I will answer You when you call. When You announce your presence, I will open the door to my heart. Come in, dearest Lord, and commune with me.

Affections of the Heart

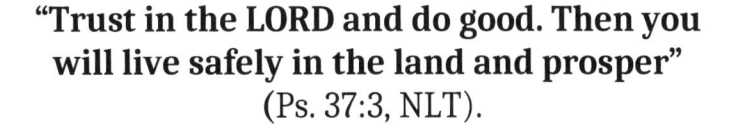

∾

"Trust in the LORD and do good. Then you will live safely in the land and prosper" (Ps. 37:3, NLT).

Often when we lose our peace and suffer from internal confusion it's due to an inner battle of affections. Who do we love more—our own desires or God? Do we allow our selfish wants to confuse us? Do we trump up reasons why we deserve certain things and get depressed when we can't figure out why?

Feeling perplexed, we ask ourselves why God would withhold those things from us. Rather than trusting the integrity of God, we struggle to understand God. It's at that place where we lose our peace and begin to entertain "vain imaginations." When we fail to trust the integrity of God, we begin to lose perspective, living in a constant state of unrest. This whirlwind of mental activity actually destroys the peace of God. At that point we feel He is a million miles away, and His manifest presence is nowhere to be found.

Whatever we love more than God creates this unrest and lack of tranquility in our souls. We must crucify any affection that causes our hearts to drift. We must share with our Lord how we feel, and why this unrest will not do. Once more we must install Him on the throne of our lives and command the whirlwind of confusion to stop.

At that place we will refuse to entertain "vain imaginations" that divide the heart and awaken carnal appetites. Instead, we choose to embrace the sweet Holy Spirit and ask Him to strengthen us where we are weak. We will strive to love Him more than our earthly affections, and to embrace the cross with dignity. We claim the mind of Christ and embrace His divine will. We run back into the secret place of His presence and throw our questions and concerns at His feet. We trust in Him alone, and when we can't trace His hands, we still choose to trust His integrity.

I must crucify any affection that causes my heart to drift away from You, Lord. I trust in Your integrity when I do not understand Your ways. I will live in peace because I know I am secure in the palm of Your hands.

Submitted Lover

"Who is this that cometh up from the wilderness, leaning upon her beloved? I raised thee up under the apple tree: there thy mother brought thee forth: there she brought thee forth that bare thee" (Song 8:5).

The Lord is searching for a Bride who will lay it all down for Him. She will not tolerate self-love or the comforts of a temporary satisfaction. She is surrendered to the glory of the Lord, enveloped by His presence, burning with the fire of His love.

She is *"leaning"* on her Beloved. Her self-life is crucified to the cause of the One she loves most so that the fire of His eyes burns in her soul.

Jesus is our model of what that kind of love looks like.

"Greater love has no one than this, than to lay down his life for his friends" (John 15:13, NKJV).

"By this we know love, because He laid down His life for us. And we ought to lay down *our* lives for the brethren" (I John 3:16, NKJV).

He laid it **all** down. He submitted himself to the "will of the Father" and willingly "laid down his life" for those He loves most. He did not love in word only, but also in deed. He took on the "form of a servant." He lived a yielded life and "humbled himself, and became obedient unto death, even death on the cross." He submitted His will for the sake of His bride.

Even so, a bridal company is being prepared "under the apple tree," learning to "lean upon her Beloved" with a selfless pursuit. This is not a mere seeking of His benefits, but His heart. She now willingly lays down self-ambition. By "taking up the cross" we are choosing consecration to the Lord in our walk with Him.

"If anyone desires to come after Me, let him deny himself, and take up his cross, and follow Me" (Matt. 16:24, NKJV).

The word "if" indicates this is a decision we ourselves must choose. We choose to die to our pride and our self-centered ways. We choose to be a "submitted lover." We choose to walk beyond the level of our present experience. The choice is ours.

"If ye love me, keep my commandments" (John 14:15).

Do we love Him the way we say we do? Are we obedient to the extent of laying it all down? If we are, He gives us a special promise:

"I will love him, and will manifest myself to him" (John 14:21b).

A personal touch from a personal God, and a divine revelation of who He is, comes to those who lay down their lives for Him. We then can cry out, "He is altogether lovely. This is my beloved, and this is my friend."

Thank you, Lord, that time after time You draw us. That Your heart is continually stirred with kindness toward us. That You desire fellowship and communion with us. You "choose" to have covenant with us. Will I choose to be a "submitted lover of Yours...?"

One Glance from His Eyes

"You have stolen my heart, my sister, my bride; you have stolen my heart *with one glance of your eyes,* with one jewel of your necklace" (Song 4:9, NIV).

Why do I believe what I believe? It can be summed up in one word—"relationship." It's not about slavishly following a long list of authoritarian rules, lest I anger God. It's all about knowing Him personally and wanting to please Him. The religious leaders in Jesus' day firmly claimed to know God, but they killed Jesus when He came to rescue mankind. Jesus unsympathetically rebuked them for their hard hearts and blatant, unrepentant hypocrisy. When we know Jesus in a personal way, we can't help but love and desire Him. In turn, we will try to obey Him because we know He has our very best interests in mind.

My dad has been a real inspiration to me. He has great integrity; I have never in all my years heard him tell a lie. He's always been honest with me, even when it hurt. I have always noticed His deep desire to really know Jesus as a friend, not merely as some historical figure. It stems from when he was fifteen years old. Let me explain.

Dad lived on the ocean in Maine. His family came from a long line of Canadian commercial fishermen. My grandmother was a deeply dedicated Christian lady who was a minister with my grandpa. She was a pastor, a Bible school professor, an inner-city relief worker who reached out to the "destitute and needy"—the "down and out." It was said of my grandmother that she never said an unkind word about anyone. I loved her so much.

One night, at age fifteen, my dad went to bed in his room. He was pondering what he should do with his life. He was wide-awake, not sleeping, when Jesus walked into his room and stood at the foot of his bed. He opened His hands to my dad, so that the nail prints were clearly evident. My dad said he had never seen such great love before. The eyes of Jesus moved Him to tears.

At that moment Dad was transformed forever. He cried all night after that because Jesus loved him so much. The eyes of Jesus told the true story; no one would be able to tell of Him otherwise. He had a personal visitation from a personal Savior. Just as the early disciples dropped what they were doing to follow Jesus, by reason of "one gaze from His eyes," after one look my dad knew what he was "called" to do. Most people do not have such awe-inspiring encounters with their physical eyes. My dad was incredibly blessed by that life-changing incident.

Turn your head, precious one; He is looking your way with eyes full of love. One look will transform your life. His head is turned toward you now. When you look at Him, you steal His heart. Can you see Him? With arms open He desires to embrace you and tenderly take you away in His presence. Take the hand of the Master, for He is waiting for you in the secret place!

A Beautiful Heart

"The King's daughter is all *glorious within*: her clothing is of wrought gold" (Ps. 45:13). (emphasis added)

This is our hour and season to be that radiant Bride, to shine forth the goodness of God. He delights in drawing close to His Bride. His eyes are always on us, and His beloved shall flourish once more—brighter, sweeter, lovelier, more beautiful, more glorious, purer, increasingly radiant, and fairer than any other! They shall carry the glorious presence of their Lord and shall flourish forever in the courts of our God! You can hear their cries from the secret place singing as one: **"Yea, he is altogether lovely"** (Song of Solomon 5:16).

Hidden deep beneath man's outer appearance is his heart. A person's heart is not always discerned because people can only see what's visible through their eyes. We often place greater value on someone who is flashy, bold and performs well. But dear friend, do you not know that inner wealth and inner beauty are far more valuable and precious to God than what we see with our eyes? From God's viewpoint, these qualities are worth far more: maturity, wisdom, character, divine revelation, and the willingness to carry the heart of God.

The wealthiest people aren't those with the most money, but rather they have the "inner wealth of the Spirit of God" dwelling inside them, knowing Him as a close friend and forever leaning upon His breast.

Inner wealth and true beauty do not come through a prayer line, but only when our stubborn nature is buried in His abounding love, where we are content to behold His loving face; where we live a yielded life, a humble heart, that yields to the Master's will, and all that remains is the brilliance of His divine nature that can now freely flow and reflect through us. Those are the qualities that make us truly wealthy.

Glorious Within

"There are many virtuous and capable women in the world, but you surpass them all! *Charm is deceptive, and beauty does not last*; but a woman who fears the Lord will be greatly praised" (Prov. 31:29-30, NLT).
(emphasis added)

According to Scripture, it's clear that outward beauty does not last. It is fleeting and quickly passes, but character endures and is a real and lasting treasure. The virtuous woman of Proverbs 31 was very beautiful. Her inner beauty was so rare that she was remembered throughout all time in Scripture. Proverbs 31 is also a prophetic view of the Bride of Christ. One that exudes an inner beauty and not just a deceptive surface charisma.

[10] "Hearken, O daughter, and consider, and incline thine ear; forget also thine own people, and thy Father's house;

[11] So shall the King greatly desire thy beauty: for he is thy Lord; and worship thou him.

¹³ The king's daughter is all glorious within: her clothing is of wrought gold." (Ps. 45:10-11, 13)

His Bride has learned to listen and obey the Lord in all things, giving Him first place. He is her first priority and her only focus. She loves Him more than life itself and radiates an inner beauty that captures the heart of her Bridegroom. The King is drawn to the true beauty of her pure heart. This golden queen is glorious; her clothing is wrought in gold. Gold speaks of His divine nature. She is beautiful in every way. She is wrapped in His presence.

The Bridegroom is so moved by her inner beauty He then cries out.

"Thou art all fair, my love; there is no spot in thee" (Song of Solomon 4:7).

He recognizes the deep work He has done inside her. The spots have been covered by His blood, and she is pure and righteous in His sight. Her character reflects the heart of God; she is beautiful in spirit.

Beautiful In Spirit

Have you ever met someone who was exquisitely beautiful in the spirit? Sometimes, you come across people so special and unique that they simply stand out. Even spending just a few minutes with them brings about a great life change. They carry a rare beauty seldom seen anywhere else. They shine forth the beauty of the Lord.

"And let the beauty of the Lord our God be upon us" (Ps. 90:17a).

There's something special about carrying a beautiful spirit. In Psalm 90, we read that we are **to let** the beauty of the Lord our God be upon us. We're to be representatives of Jesus—those who allow the beauty of the Holy Spirit to shine through us to change the world.

Some people carry something very rare and special, and I've asked myself a million times how they received it and how it came about. We know that we're to be a manifest representation of the Lord on Earth, an expression of our Father's heart, so others may be transformed when touched by the presence of the Lord within us. Don't you want others to leave a conversation with you knowing they've been changed? I readily admit that occasionally I've sat with such great men and women of God, that my life was altered in an instant, never to be the same again!

Their examples also created a divine hunger in me to run hard after God. The humility and beauty they carried are scarcely seen—rare and precious. They had a depth that goes far deeper than what I see in most believers. But that's the thing—you and I are not called to be normal, average, or status quo Christians, but to be carriers of the beauty of the Lord, to be His radiant Bride.

What does it mean to let the beauty of the Lord be upon us? What kind of **qualities** do people see when they see Jesus in us? I know it when I see it, I know it when I hear it, but I had to ask the Lord about it because I'd never heard anyone talk about it. What is the beauty of the Lord?

The Lord is looking for a remnant Bride who not only functions in the gifts of the Spirit, but appreciates the stunning attributes of God, and lives to reflect His beautiful character in **love, joy,**

peace, patience, kindness, goodness, faithfulness, gentleness and self-control.

One person, in particular, did fit that description, though she's now with the Lord. Her name was Hattie Hammond, and she was an evangelist far ahead of her time. I hadn't even listened to her sermons yet; I had only read her 50 sermon titles, but that was enough to quicken my spirit, sensing the beauty and presence of the Lord that she carried so well. When I finally listened to her messages, she called out to the Lover of her soul, and such beauty came forth. When she spoke, it came from the depths of her heart. The beauty of the Lord truly rested upon her, so I asked the Lord, "What caused the beauty of the Lord to rest upon her life?"

The late Wade Taylor was another of these remarkable people who radiated a quiet kindness and beauty. I loved to phone him because he was always happy to hear from me. It meant a great deal just to hear the tender compassion in his voice. When he ministered, you could feel the Spirit and the Life emanating from his messages.

Spiritual fathers to Wade Taylor were Walter Beuttler and John Wright Follette, others in whom a humble, holy beauty and anointing resided.

These great mothers and fathers of the faith have inspired my walk with God so much that they propelled me forward to seek the Lord and His beauty. In my pursuit, I now know that the Father desires to raise up a Bride who carries the exquisite beauty of the Lord, so others will see it and become eager to receive that same special touch of the Lord.

The Lord is raising a **mature Bride of Jesus Christ** (Rev. 19:7-9). She is prepared and ready to assume her position in the Kingdom. She is enveloped by the atmosphere of heaven, and the beauty of the Lord rests upon her. When others see her, they see Jesus. She's been so long with the Master that she begins to radiate the very glory of His presence. Yes, it's getting darker today. Yes, there still seem to be places that are not open to the move of the Spirit, but He is raising a remnant Bride who carries the beauty of the Lord, changing the atmosphere as she walks into a room, no matter where she goes. This is our hour and season to be that radiant Bride, to shine forth the goodness of God.

Many believers are chasing after ministry opportunities. You see, they're waiting for the next big chance to grace the cover of a well-known Christian publication. It's all about self-promotion and becoming popular. Let me declare boldly that it's far more essential to know Jesus and carry His beauty than to become the next big thing in our Christian circles.

Let me ask, how do we reflect the beauty of the Lord? I wrote about this in *The Beauty of the Lord: Keys to Radiating the Glory of God* (2018). I will give you the short version here, and I want the Lord to continue to give you revelation about this even after you finish reading this.

2 Corinthians 3:18: **"But we all with open face beholding as in a glass the glory of the Lord are changed into that same image from glory to glory even as by the Spirit of the Lord."**

The New Living Translation says, **"So, all of us who have had their veil removed can see and reflect the glory of the Lord and the Lord who is the Spirit makes us more and more like him *as we are changed into his glorious image*"** (emphasis added).

Do you want the beauty of the Lord to rest upon you? **Be with Jesus! Spend so much time with your friend Jesus that His image is burned upon your soul.** Then, spend more time basking in His presence and resting in His glory the way

Samuel did in the tabernacle. Spend time waiting on the Lord, and He will renew you so that you will look just like Him, and His fragrance and beauty will be all over you!

Spend time beholding him—I love that phrase, **beholding the Lord.** To behold Him is to soak, rest, and dwell in His manifest presence. To behold Him is to steadily gaze in His eyes of fervent love that blaze like fire and can't help but transform you. Behold the Lord, and as you do, He will capture your heart, and you will be changed, so you reflect His image from glory to glory.

Also, wait. Just when you think you've arrived, you'll find that there's a whole other realm to enter. During this time, He'll allow difficult people to refine you and help you to know you still need Him, now more than ever. His Bride will walk through many desert places, but this will lead to a spiritually wealthy place where she will flourish.

Don't let yourself be discouraged; just spend time in His presence. I love taking walks with my sweet wife, Diane; we enjoy being together. Do you share those sacred moments with the Lord too? Do you love being with Him? Some of the most precious moments can happen when you sit on a bench and do nothing except enjoy each other's company.

You don't even have to say "I love you." Just keep silent, and love Him as you realize that your love for the Lord is real and genuine, and unbelievably, He loves you even more.

Beautiful In Heart

The most beautiful people in the world may never make the *Who's Who* list or be counted among the popular crowd. However, that inner glow of gentle beauty shines brightly for all to see if they care enough to search deeper. A truly beautiful soul has fought the good fight and does not give up. These people know the bitter taste of defeat but have persevered anyway. They lost their fair share of battles but kept on going. They faced the fierce winds of pain and agony, the dark nights of the soul, and the wilderness of loneliness and rejection. But once they came out of the pit, they were filled with deep compassion and a fresh appreciation for the Lord. Their hearts overflow with compassion and empathy for others who suffer, as the fight has produced an inner beauty that captures the attention of heaven. A beautiful heart is precious in God's Kingdom; in fact, it is a truly rare and valuable treasure that will be evident to all those who have eyes to see.

His Bride knows how to behold the Lord and sit before Him; they lie at His feet and stay there until they are transformed into His likeness. The people who once knew them no longer recognize them. Their personality is radically altered; they talk less and love God more. He gives them His gifts and power because they prove themselves to be trustworthy with the deep heart of God.

Beautiful people don't just happen. They are molded in the presence of the King. This is our hour and season to be that radiant, beautiful Bride, to shine forth with the goodness of God. His Bride is beautiful inside and out; she has obtained favor in heaven. Her display of inner wealth is worth far more than any jewel. She has obtained the boundless treasure of a beautiful heart. What more could we ask for?

Lord, give me the boundless treasure of a beautiful heart. The greatest wealth I seek is the inner wealth of spirit. May I carry a beautiful heart that comes from one that values the intimate whispers from the holy Throne.

How Will You Be Remembered? (1)

"By faith Enoch was taken from this life, so that he did not experience death: "He could not be found, because God had taken him away. For before he was taken, he was commended as one who pleased God" (Heb. 11:5, NIV). (emphasis added)

I often ponder how short life is. Many times, I walk through cemeteries and read the headstones of those who've gone before. I scan the theme note of each person's life summed up with a short description. Some say, "Good Father," or "Faithful," while others read "Loving Husband," or "Loved God." Entire generations of people have gone on to their eternal reward, and their lives are summed up with a single short statement. These generations deserve our respect.

There are some stones that let me know their owners are not in heaven. This bothers me a great deal. In fact, it compels me to share the gospel with a lost world. How many in the cemetery are not with the Lord? Only God knows. Some are in eternal torment, and I lose sleep over such knowledge. It's too late for them, but there is yet hope for those who still live.

As I scan these stones, the last remnants of people's lives, I often wonder, *how will I be remembered?* I wonder if a young person will pass by my gravestone one day and if so, what will they read? What legacy will I leave my children and my grandchildren and their children? In this day of technology our lives are forever digitally stored. Many generations of the past are gone and the stories of their lives lost. Many loved ones cannot tell you much beyond the past three or four generations. But today, if the Lord is to tarry, our lives will be viewed by future generations. Videos, pictures, and sound bites will be stored for review by future generations. What will they learn from us?

Something compels me to press on toward the mark. Not only does my future reward depend on it, but I am also creating my legacy right now. Walking through a cemetery reminds me of this startling fact. What will be said about my life? How will I go down in history? No one will remember whether we were rich or poor, famous or not. The only thing we take with us is our salvation and the souls we've won to Christ.

Nothing drives me to my knees faster than the thought of walking out my faith to my children. I want to be "Jesus with skin on" to them. I want to be remembered as a man who walked with God like Enoch did. I desire to know my God as a close friend and lover. That desire brings the tears to my eyes and compels me forward, even when I feel like I can't manage another step. I want to be remembered as a "friend of God," and "one who loved his family faithfully." Each choice I make in life determines whether or not this will be said of me.

We all make mistakes, but rather than condemning ourselves when we blow it, we must ask forgiveness and get back up again to keep pressing on. Will we have tenacious faith? Will we give ourselves to prayer and fasting? Will we pay the price to be that "friend of God" who will so encourage future generations? Life passes quickly, and before we know it we'll go on to eternity. At that moment, people will pause to ponder the meaning of our lives. With that coming evaluation in mind, we must create a worthwhile legacy now for generations following. It humbles me and brings me to tears to realize my short, simple life could encourage a future traveler. It creates such a sense of responsibility.

Legacy

As sometimes a youth enters a dense wood
And carefully leaves stone markings along his path
Lest he get lost.
So also, I desire to mark the trail of my life
With clear signposts to the Father's House,
That no one following in my footsteps
Will ever stumble or be made weak
Or worse, lose their way.
Lord let my life be a beacon light
For travelers coming after me.

----Steve Porter

Lord, please use my little life for Your glory. Let me be a shining example of one who paid the price to be Your friend. Let my life count for something! Let me encourage the faith of others through my obedience.

How Will You Be Remembered? (2)

"After removing Saul, he made David their king. God testified concerning him: 'I have found David son of Jesse, a man after my own heart; he will do everything I want him to do" (Acts 13:22). (emphasis added)

When we breathe our last on earth, we will enter our eternal reward with sweat still on our brows. As we push and press on toward the mark, our committed lives will count for something in heaven. Yes, it is important to create a legacy for future generations, but this question is most important of all: When we stand before God what will He have to say about us?

It seems like a faraway event, that **Judgment Seat of Christ,** yet it's much closer than we think. On that day, will we hear those precious words, "Well done, thou good and faithful servant"? If we haven't lived life well or if we have not been faithful, God will not lie. Instead of "Well done" we will hear "Well, what do you have to say for yourself?" This scene has been replayed in my spirit many times, standing before my God. This creates such a holy and healthy fear of Him; it compels me to shake off apathy and self-love. It reminds me not to let my heart drift away from Him.

One day I will walk through the throne room and stand before God who will review my life. When I look into the face of my beautiful Savior, I want Him to be pleased with me! I want Him to embrace me as a friend. I want our meeting on that day to be a great reunion between beloved companions. But I must determine today whether that will be a reality. Good intentions are simply not enough!

It's only through the grace of God we are made righteous. It is not *"by works, lest we should boast."* However, we should cultivate *"fruit that remains."* Shrugging off apathy we should resist a comfortable complacency that would deceive us into believing "we can rest on our laurels." Beware of a drifting heart!

Our prime goal, our strongest endeavor, should be to make Him our closest friend. When we make mistakes, we must run in repentance into the forgiving arms of a gracious Savior. As we continue to climb the narrow way, with sweat still on our brows, we enter eternity to be embraced by our

Lord. How I long to see my Savior and friend face to face!

*Yes, it is important to create a legacy for future generations, but most of all what will **You** say about our lives when we stand before you? Lord, I want You to say "Well done, thou good and faithful servant!"*

Final Reckoning

What measure of my life shall be
When weighed in God's eternity?
What shall be counted on that day
While I have walked this earthly way?
Not judgment for conformity
To shallow Christianity
Not lip assent to truths half-heard
Nor failure to obey your Word
Not living for myself alone
And hoarding seeds I should have sown.
When books are open to review
Parading deeds I can't undo
What shall your verdict say of me?
Idolatry or constancy?
A life well lived and when it's done
A crown, dear Lord, that I have won?
I pray upon my balance sheet
This crown to cast down at your feet
I pray the sum of all my days
When weighed will earn my Master's praise
That when I trade "the here" for "there"
"A Christ one" is the name I'll bear!

----Marie Lawson

The Whisper of God

"Ah, I hear him—my lover! Here he comes, leaping on the mountains and bounding over the hills" (Song 2:8, TLB).

"My dove in the clefts of the rock, in the hiding places on the mountainside, show me your face, let me hear your voice; for your voice is sweet, and your face is lovely" Song 2:14, NIV).

Hearing Whispers from the Throne Room

Have you really heard the whisper of God? How He speaks so softly to those He loves! Many times we walk away from His face, and our ears are not tuned to the Father's heart. His whisper can really change our lives. *"He stands at the door and knocks,"* wanting to whisper to us: *"Come away with me, My Love."*

Many have followed in the "footsteps of the flock," walking down a beaten path lit by the life lanterns of those who have come before us.

In Genesis 3:8 Adam and Eve walked with God in the "cool of the evening," listening ever so closely to the whisper of God in the Garden. Enoch walked with God for nearly four centuries. Moses knew Him—"face-to-face and mouth-to-mouth," as man speaks to a friend. He was tuned to the whisper of a close companion. Abraham was also "the friend of God," and Samuel was very young when he recognized the sound of God's voice. David was "a man after God's own heart." He sat on a faraway hill singing melodies in his young shepherd's heart. He knew His Father's whisper as he "entered the courts of the Lord," and wrote the Psalms. John the Beloved heard the whisper. How could he not gently lay his head upon the breast of Jesus?

You may be wondering, "Why is God so quiet?"

Isaiah 45:15 says this: "You are a God that hides Yourself."

God is silent so you will seek for Him. How much do you really want to hear His whisper? Is it just a fleeting thought or is it a beat from your very heart? You see, God is not distant. He is close enough to hear your heartbeat and say your name. You might even ask yourself this question: "If God seems distant, guess who moved?"

We lose everything if we don't hear His voice. One time on a prayer walk the Lord said, *"I'm a 'Just Because' God! Come to me, Steve, just because."* God is looking for a friend who comes to Him "just because." Not for what is in His hands but to hear a whisper coming from His love-filled heart. The whisper of God makes one hear the heart of God.

His whisper brings many helpful things in our lives:

1) God's whisper brings correction. Ex. 4:10-11
2) God's whisper brings inspiration. Jer. 1:5-8
3) God's whisper brings instruction. Isa. 6:5-9
4) God's whisper brings revelation. 1 Cor. 2:10

When does God whisper?

He speaks when you're quiet—hush your soul and listen.

He speaks when you are still. Ps. 46:10

He speaks when you're ready—anticipate Him.

Lord, You hold Your bride close to You. You embrace me, whispering in my ear, and revealing Your intentions toward me. Your whisper is not a matter of sound or volume, I keep my ear tuned to the Father's voice. I will even move beyond hearing Your whisper to listening for the yearning of Your very heart.

Manifest

"He that has My commandments, and keeps them, he it is that loves Me: and he that loves Me shall be loved of My Father, and I will love him, and will manifest Myself to him" (John 14:21, NKJV).

The truth is that the Lord loves everyone, yet not everyone regularly experiences His manifest presence. There are two requirements for experiencing the abiding presence I speak of: submitted **love** and **obedience.** He desires to manifest Himself, but are we willing to yield to His love and obey Him even when it hurts? *The Pulpit Commentary,* referring to *Thayer's Greek Lexicon*, says that this word "manifest" means the Lord will make himself "personally real." Thus, Jesus is saying, *"I will plainly show myself to him."*

Isn't it remarkable that it's even possible for us to "experience" the personal presence of God in our lives? God yearns to manifest his presence to all, but He can do so only when those who love Him act in obedience to Him.

Jesus asks us to prove our love for God by keeping His Commandments. If we love Him, we act on His words and as the Father sees those acts of love, He responds with divine love and a revelation of Himself.

If you and I love Him enough He will manifest His presence to us. Then we can position ourselves in places where His manifest presence can spill over and touch the hearts of others. People have done this at various times in church history, and we usually find a revival or an outpouring breaking out as a result.

He isn't telling us how to earn anything; He's showing us the way we can discover Him. When God hides, it's because He wants to see if we really want to go after Him. Is this desire for His presence just a fleeting impulse or is there a genuine hunger for Him? Those who are willing to risk everything to run after Him through obedience really desire Him, and God, in turn, will manifest Himself to them. He knows He can trust them with His very heart and will therefore, come for sweet fellowship.

Father, manifest Yourself to me! I want to know You. I love You enough to listen and act on what You say! Help me to live and dwell in Your manifest presence all the days of my life. I know You long to manifest Your presence in my life.

Being Lifted into a Higher Realm

"I slept but my heart was awake. Listen! My lover is knocking..." (Song 5:2, NIV)

"After these things I looked, and behold, a door *standing* open in heaven. And the first voice which I heard *was* like a trumpet speaking with me, saying, *"Come up here, and I will show you things which must take place after this."* Immediately I was in the Spirit..."
(Rev. 4:1-2a, NKJV)

I was sitting across the table from a prophet from South Africa. We were having dinner together in Cape Town, South Africa after a long weekend of ministry. I had just spoken at a conference there, and the Lord had given me a special word for him and his wife. I remember seeing a flame of fire going over this dear brother and his wife as we prayed. I could sense the manifest presence as I spoke over him. This prophetic word had been building up inside of me all day and when I released it this dear couple was visibly shaken by the presence of the precious Holy Spirit.

At dinner he turned to me and I knew he had shifted gears into the prophetic realm and a presence was released as he spoke into my life. "The Lord will open your eyes and ears to see and hear into the spirit realm like never before. This trip to South Africa is an important season in your ministry, where God is lifting you into higher realms of the spirit." Before he even finished speaking, I was lost in His presence, and I knew deep inside that this word was taking me higher. As this prophet wept, I was transformed, and God was doing a deep work inside me that night at the dinner table.

The journey home from South Africa was exhausting. An eleven-hour flight to Frankfurt, Germany seemed endless, with yet another eight-hour flight to Washington DC, before a final leg to Pittsburgh, Pennsylvania. I almost wished I'd taken the direct route home from Johannesburg to Atlanta, but the idea of a seventeen-hour nonstop flight had seemed too overwhelming. Once home, I collapsed into my bed after hugging my family for the one-hundredth time. Quickly I was asleep, but my heart was still awake to the things of the Spirit. I knew something had been activated through that prayer at the dinner table.

I began to dream, but it felt so real, I couldn't tell reality from my dream. An angel of the Lord appeared to me in my dream and stood there in majestic splendor. The holiness of God was surrounding him, and the atmosphere of heaven was being released. He had come from the very throne room of God. Instantly I knew he had something to share with me. I began to follow him down a hallway and suddenly I was airborne. I was no longer walking but was lifted above the floor, guided by an unseen hand.

We approached a staircase, and I became aware that I was going to fly over the rails. I was nervous but said, "I must have faith." I looked down once I passed the rails and noticed I was standing above the stairs several hundred feet below me. All fear immediately left as I fully trusted in the Lord to protect me. My feet slowly landed in a room and the Angel began to instruct me. I was taken to other rooms, where I learned new things in each room I visited. My eyes and ears were open to see and hear into the spirit realm like never before.

All at once I woke, but didn't want to move, as a powerful presence of God was still lingering in the room. I replayed my dream over and over again in my heart. Through this dream the Lord reminded me of the prophetic word I received in South

Africa. He also gave me a corporate message for the church illustrated by my dream.

I believe the Lord is saying He desires to lift **the Body of Christ** into a higher realm of the spirit—that we as His treasured Bride have the potential to rise into much greater levels of understanding regarding the deeper things of God. We must have faith in God alone to trust that He will lift us higher, rather than trusting in our own abilities. He will also be faithful to lead us from place to place on special assignment, letting us see and hear what the Spirit is saying and desiring in a particular moment in time. We will then speak the heart of God to those who have not yet come into the Holy of Holies. A hunger will be created in their hearts to also seek after God. In our day there is a great need for those who can hear the whispers of God.

I am completely in love with You, dear Jesus. I will never be the same. I am taken by Your love for me. What kind of love can reach so deep? You see through me, You know my name, You know my heart. Your love for me is unquenchable, You move my soul. You're so beautiful to me I can scarcely put it into words...The fragrance of Your love is a sweet perfume. I will pour it back upon You. The things that distract will not hold me back. I hear Your tender whispers coming from Your throne, I see the light coming from Your chambers. I walk in and rest awhile in the beauty of Your manifest presence.

Until Tomorrow

Reader and friend—even as these written impartations find their ending—the loving messages from the heart of our Father continue. Impossible as it may seem for some to realize, the magnificent Sovereign of the Universe avidly desires to reveal Himself to us.

Hungry, thirsting soul, go deeper, higher! Your persistent, earnest seeking will give you privileged access to the throne room of Almighty God! Look for Him to invade the ordinary passage of your days. Listen intently for His voice in the still watches of the night. As you place your own will on the altar and seek Him with all your might—He will show you an awesome entryway into a superior dimension of living. The "news of the day" will become the "prophecies of tomorrow." Your heavenly download will be indescribably awesome! **The voice of the Spirit** will be louder than the shouts of the world. Your ears and your heart will hear those precious whispers from His throne.

Bride of Christ—while there is still a little while to prepare, we must look well to our adornment—our wedding garment. Let us bask now in the love and empowerment of the Master, lest we behold Him as a stranger when He comes. We will grow ever more beautiful as we take on the transforming glory of His presence. As we seek deeper depths and higher heights in Him we'll be clothed with the brilliance of the light of God!

Virgins of our living Lord, arise! Let the healing oil of the Holy Spirit pour out from your lanterns upon the hopeless and desperate in our world. Love those lost ones floundering in emptiness and confusion, as He loves them and gave Himself a sacrifice and a ransom for many.

The Bridegroom comes—He is even at the door. There will be a "wedding supper" as He promised. We are invited and we must be ready!

My Lord

In the circle of your love—in the chapel of your presence, I bask in the awesome privilege of hearing Your voice. Thank You for your holy visitations and Your divine outpourings, not only for my own life, but also for insight and encouragement for my brothers and sisters in this precious family you call Your Body. Lover of my soul, thank You for using me through this book as Your messenger!

Bonus section
Prayers of the Heart
Intimate Prayers from a Love-struck Bride

By Steve Porter

Note: Below are "fervent prayers of the heart". Please pray along with them, even speaking them out loud, pouring out your heart to Him.

The Lifting

Father, lift me up! Lift me above the circumstances that try to hold me down. Lift me above the attempts of the enemy to rob me of my peace and joy. Cancel out any trick he uses to place a wet blanket of worry and defeat over my life. Instead, cover me with the warm comforter of Your manifest presence. Lift me up Lord, above these temporary contrary winds, and let me ride on the wings of Your glory. Father, may I see things from Your point of view and not from my limited earthly view. Higher, higher, higher, Lord! Oh, to see what You see, to hear what You hear, to feel what You feel. Hold me close when I do not know what to do nor where to go. Most of all, lift me into Your arms where I will find divine rest.

Re-Clothe Me

The Lord desires to re-clothe us, taking off our independent, self-assertive, all-knowing attitudes and clothing us with humility, dependence, and a meek and contrite heart.

Father, we need a change of clothes! Remove our filthy rags of pride, ego, and selfishness, and clothe us with the beauty of the Lord. Father, Father, may the world not see us, but You. May Your glory shine forth in such a way that others will see the difference and run to Your cross, desiring You more than life itself.

Jesus, sweet Master, rule and reign in my life to such an extent that all my self-centered ways would die, replaced by a deeper yielding. I want to be that city set on a hill that cannot be hidden. May Your beauty shine through me! Re-clothe me and transform me; this is my prayer today.

Captivate

Awaken my passion for only You. Captivate my heart again, oh God. Let Your waves of love splash over and drench my very being. May Your face be continually before me. When I reach out in Your direction, You quickly embrace me. I'm surrounded by Your presence. I'm speechless when I behold Your beauty. I'm overcome by Your compassion. Oh, precious Lord, You melt my heart with only one gaze from Your eyes. You are altogether lovely. I am Yours and You are mine.

I Press

Dear Lord, I desire to press on toward the mark, to pursue the high calling of knowing You personally. Father, whatever the enemy throws at me to slow down my progress, stop him in his tracks. Halt his efforts to sidetrack and detour me. I press in today. I pursue You no matter what resistance I feel. I refuse to go by my feelings. I run toward Your loving arms holding back nothing. I pursue You with all my heart, soul and mind. I am in desperate need of You, my Jesus. I must know You. I choose to overcome any obstacle in my path that I may have the pleasure of Your company. I press in day by day. I take a hold of Your arm as I lean on You. No turning back, Lord. No turning back.

Extravagant Love

As the world gets colder, let our hearts get hotter for You, sweet Master. Faint-hearted, lukewarm love for You will never do! We don't want a cold, dead, lifeless, shallow religion; that will make us sick. I want my heart red HOT for You. Your eyes that blaze like fire bring fervent love! I run into Your arms today and lay aside all else, that I may know You! I can feel the burn of extravagant love today. Turn it up, my JESUS!

Release Movement

Beautiful King of Glory. Release movement over us in our sleep tonight, Lord! Open up the floodgates of the glory of God. Let it cover the earth! Let it fill me. Yes, yes, do it even now!

Let Me Love

Lord, let me love like Jesus does. Where I am weak, make me strong. Where I am blind, let me see, that I may function in not only Your gifts but Your fruit. Make me like You! I desperately need You to mold me into a vessel of honor that carries the beauty of Your presence. Do Your deep work in me that I may please You in all that I do.

Pen of a Skillful Writer

Father, teach our tongues what to say today, guide our words that we, Your precious people, will hear Your heartbeat. That our tongues would be like the pen of a skillful writer. Teach us what to say and how to say it. Let us sustain others with a word from You. Guide that pen, and write a story of hope that will lift someone out of the pit of the enemy and into Your presence. Do it through me today, Lord.

> **My heart overflows with a good theme;**
> **I address my psalm to the King.**
> **My tongue is like the pen of a skillful writer.**
> (Ps. 45:1, AMP)

I Want to Be a Son

Lord, before any ministry or title, I so want to be called a "son." I want to lay at Your feet and offer up my all. Father, I give You my calling, my gifts, my all, that I may *know* You. I lay any reward or crown at Your humble feet that I may *know* You! In this life the greatest place I can be is at Your feet to truly *know* You! You know me and the depths of who I am. Let me discover the depths of who You are, that I may be a true son and friend.

Pearl of Great Price

Lord, You are the Pearl of great price! Oh, how I seek Your face like hidden treasure. How I long for Your courts. Father, I am completely lovestruck. I cannot start my day without stopping to acknowledge Your greatness and Your deep and abiding love. I long to be in Your presence, under Your shadow every hour of every day, hearing Your desires, and moving in harmony with Your Spirit. My heart longs for You like a dry and thirsty land where there is no rain. To me You are more valuable than rubies and more costly than gold. Let me come and spend some time with You, for that is the only place I long to be, now and always.

Hear My Prayer

I love You and worship You. I adore You and call out to You today. I cry out with all my heart, mind and strength. I call out Your name, Jesus! Jesus, come. I seek Your face and look to You. I come not wanting anything for myself, but just to spend time in Your presence. I make room for You. I invite You into my heart. I invite You into my life. Let me decrease, that You may increase within me. Come, my Lord, and spend time with me. Take my heart as I offer it up to You. I just want more of You and to know You in ways I've never known You before. Draw me into Your presence, Lord, and I will run after You! This is my humble prayer. I just want You! In the matchless name of Jesus, I pray. Amen.

We Invite You to Come in and Rest in Our Secret Garden of Prayers

To the one who's altogether lovely, Jesus, we declare to You today that we love You with all our hearts. We thank You, dear Lord, that You are active in our lives, moving and doing that deeper work. Move in the heart of Your Beautiful bride, stirring us that we may run after You. Bring us into Your inner chambers, dear Father.

Lord, we so desire that You draw us. We invite You to come in and rest in our secret garden of prayers. We know that You're here, but we ask that You manifest Yourself even more.

Come and stir us, quicken us. Father, I know that I'm weak without You, and so I'm leaning upon You. Draw me that I may run after You. Take me by the hand into the depths of Your very chambers to discover Your beautiful heart.

Footsteps

Oh Lord, I can hear Your footsteps quietly approaching me. I can smell the sweet fragrance of fresh flowers in Your garden. It is the sweet aroma of Your manifest presence. I know You are at the gate, and You are coming my way. Come closer, oh Lord. Come closer. Don't hesitate, please come. I know You've been wounded in the past by those who have bid You come, but were no longer there when You walked into that sacred place. I promise I will wait. I will wait on You. For You are worth the wait. I willingly throw away my watch and lay down my phone. I am here waiting, and my heart burns with passionate love for You, the one I adore. Sweet Master, I bid You come.

The Table

The table is set, the door is opened wide. Oh Lord, I desire to come and dine with You. To feast on Your presence. I see You sitting there at our table, where You are content and happy that I am there with You. You have found the one whom Your soul loves, and I have found my greatest treasure in You. My Beloved, let us eat and drink of love for only our sweet communion will satisfy me. From the depths of my heart, I long and yearn for more of You. I sit at Your table with delight in this holy moment. Thank You for inviting me to dine at the Master's table this very night. I will often return to visit You here. I pledge to You my very life and love, and receive my portion of Your spirit and holy life.

Spiritual Capacity

Oh, heavenly Father. My Daddy God. Enlarge my capacity to receive more of You. I desire more of You, as only You can satisfy the deepest longings of my heart. Enlarge my portion, oh God, that I may receive more from the depths of Your chambers, that I may receive more from the depths of Your very heart. For the things of the world do not satisfy me; the wells of the world are always dry and leave me thirsty for the living water. This world has nothing to offer me. It is only You that I desire. Enlarge my capacity to receive more from Your deep, deep wells. You have created me for more. Father, why do I try to satisfy that inner thirst with things that can clearly not satisfy? Why don't I place the better waters on my lips? I move beyond the old wells of yesterday and I place my face into the living river of life and drink this large meal freely, oh Lord, that I may drink more of You.

Draw Me

Draw me into Your heart; pull me into the depths that I may truly know You. Let us run together hand-in-hand that we may approach the door to Your chambers. It is in this place where the King dwells with His manifest presence and fills the secret place. For within Your chambers is the very holy of holies and I will therefore take off my shoes and declare that the ground is holy as You are holy. I will lie at Your feet and allow my heart to release the sweet aroma of my adoration and worship.

Full Bloom

The fragrance of Your presence is sweet and pleasing. Your garden is in full bloom. In Your presence is where I long to be. Lord, bring me into Your heart. Your ways are kind and Your discipline and truth reveal Your great love. Father, show me the right way, and do not allow me to go off the path. Keep me in the truth and pull me back onto the narrow way that I may live the deeper life found only in Your presence.

No Other Name

There is no other name like Yours, for Your name is like flowing anointing oil. When I speak the syllables of Your name my heart is moved; when I say Your name my tears freely fall. I've come to know You as my closest friend, for Your name has power! Even the demons tremble, terrified of the power of Your name. No wonder the true Bride of Christ loves You so much when they say Your name. For Your name has all power and authority; only Your name can save, heal, restore and deliver. I just say Your name over and over again, and I am drawn into Your heart. Sweet Lord, my heart is always awake to hear Your tender reply.

Throw Yourself Into His Arms

I throw myself into Your arms of love, oh Lord, for You are standing there with arms open wide, waiting for me to return home to You. To me You are a great shepherd who is calling to his lost sheep. You leave the ninety-nine just to go after me. I am not alone. I am not abandoned. I am not rejected. I am Your lost little lamb, confused, heartbroken and afraid. But here You come moving on the mountain toward me. You soothe me with Your loving affection as You place me on Your shoulders and carry me home. You are my beacon of hope; I am not left to make it on my own. I am Your child and in You I place all my hope. Thank You, oh Father, for carrying me safely home.

Eye of The Dove

The doorway of Your heart is calling me to come higher. I will not wait. I will not offer excuses nor will I be distracted. My eyes are focused on You, for You have given me singular vision—the eye of the dove to only see You. Please reach for my hand and pull me into that secret place as I yield my heart to You. Stop the enemy and his little foxes from spoiling our love. Kiss me with the kisses of Your presence while You unveil my understanding of Your holy Word. Come with a visitation just for me. For I need You and want You and compel You to come. Hidden stairs call me up into the higher realms of Your vast and beautiful heart. No doubts or fears can stop my climb into Your chambers, my King.

The Hidden Revealed

I need Your love and Your affectionate kiss that I may be prepared for the days ahead, that I may know the strategies of war when the day of battle comes upon me; for when I dwell in Your courts You expose the truth. All of it. Your secrets, Your strategies, even the hidden mysteries are revealed with the kiss of Your presence. Don't hold anything back. Reveal and download Your truth within me that my hands may be trained for war, that my feet will be ready to hold fast on solid ground. Speak to me the divine tactics I need to make the enemy flee away in stunned panic. Yes, divine Lord, Your kiss leads to all these things and more. Therefore, I need that kiss more than life itself for it is in that face-to-face encounter that the obscurities of this life will become transparent and bring true life.

Hidden Forest

Our resting place, oh God, is perfumed with Your presence, and it is like a garden flourishing in the center of a hidden forest. Flowers of rare beauty are planted from our many visits there. Each time I leave the garden better off. Oh, divine Master, would You not touch my heart, that I may not place anything before You, that You would be to me as sweet as I am to You. Let Your face shine upon me that I may behold You in Your glory. Let Your glory expose any darkness in me, revealing any wicked way that would hinder our relationship. With adoration I behold You, on bended knee I lay it all at Your feet. May my life be pliable in Your hands that through the fire I will be preserved and come forth as gold.

New Beginnings

Dear Lord, You are the God of new beginnings. It is You who gives us grace to start over and pursue You again with all of our hearts. I want nothing to hinder or stop the Holy Spirit flow in my life. I yearn for the deep things of the Spirit, allowing the Holy Spirit to move more freely in my life. I leave behind the old man and the old ways of doing things and I pursue righteousness, holiness and purity in my life. May the totality of my being be surrendered over to You. May this place of yielding and dying to self not be short-lived but last all the days of my life. I need You, Lord. I need a Holy Spirit infusion of Power and Presence that I would respect You always and stand in awe of Your holiness. Lord, I am trusting for a new beginning, another outpouring, and a fresh start today. Thank You, Jesus, that You are mine and I am Yours forever.

The Fullness

Lord, teach me to wait on You. Teach me how to be silent in Your presence. Cause me to listen in the stillness rather than to fall into the chaotic and the busy storms of life. Cause me to pray with a believing heart that You will do as You have promised because You are a rewarder of those who diligently seek You. Out of that seeking will come a sweetness in Your presence that will bring me fullness of joy as well as fullness of everything that I need, for there is a fire within me that grows. This fire is fanned by the genuine desire to come away with You in the quiet, oh Lord. May I not burn with activity that will only lead to barrenness. Put out that flame of busyness that I may learn to wait on You, to behold You, to know You, to do well in Your presence, oh God. Whatever state that I am in I pray that I be content, that my soul becomes quiet, that the whirlwind of thoughts that hold my mind hostage will be calmed, that I would cease from all human effort and learn to be quiet, that I would hold before You a believing heart that would relish the time of sacred moments as I seek the Lord.

Dear Reader,

If your life was touched while reading "Whispers from the Throne Room" please let us know! We would love to celebrate with you! Please visit our website. www.findrefuge.tv

Consumed by His Presence,
Steve Porter

About the Author

Steve and his wife Diane founded Refuge Ministries and a presence-driven publishing company, Deeper Life Press. Steve has written many books and has a special anointing to bring forth the deep truths of the Spirit with a clarity and simplicity that draws one into a closer walk and a deeper relationship with our Lord Jesus Christ. Steve's books, tracts, articles, and videos have touched countless lives around the world.

Deeper Life
PRESS

More Books by Steve & Diane Porter

Garden of The Heart- *Healing Letters to Ladies (Diane Porter)*
Crocodile Meat- *New and Extended Version (Steve's Life Story)*
Crocodile Meat- *Student Version*
Whispers from the Throne Room- *Reflections on the Manifest Presence*
Limitless
He Leads Me Beside Still Waters- *50 Love Letters of Healing and Restoration from Our Lord*
Streams in the Desert- *Healing Letters for the Wounded Heart*
Invading the Darkness- *Power Evangelism Training 101*
Pearls of His Presence- *Intimate Devotions for the Spiritually Hungry*
The Tongue of the Learned- *How to Flow in the Prophetic Anointing*
Draw Me- *The Deep Cry of the Bride*
The Beauty of the Lord- *Your Keys to Radiating the Glory of God*
Hidden Treasure- *Intimate Devotions for the Spiritually Hungry*

Daniel Nash- *Laborer with Finney. Mighty in Prayer*

His Hands Extended- *Stories of Love at the Nursing Home* (Diane Porter)

Reflections for a Deeper Life

The Way of the Master- *A Teaching Tale and More*

Musing of a Watchman- A Compilation of Spiritual Writings- Volume 1

Musing of a Watchman- A Compilation of Spiritual Writings- Volume 2

<u>**Coming in 2022 by Steve & Diane Porter**</u>

The Great Holiness Revival is Coming!- *The Magnificent Beauty of His Holiness*

Thirsty Waters- *Intimate Devotions for the Spiritually Hungry*

All Creation Testifies

*Bulk orders and international orders are available upon request. Email for details or order directly online.

> "My Child, you are weeping at My feet..."

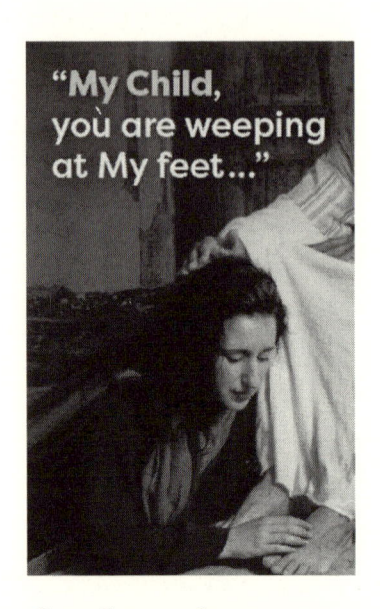

(Pamphlets for those that want to go deeper spiritually)

Spiritual Maturity Tracts by Steve Porter now available!

See our website

www.findrefuge.tv

(THE BRIDE OF CHRIST BOOK SERIES)

by Steve Porter

Please pray for me as I work hard on this special trilogy series. I so desire this special series to lift the church into the inner chambers of the King!

1. Draw Me-The Deep Cry of the Bride **(Now Available)**

2. Christ's Golden Queen-A Prophetic View of Psalms 45
(Coming in 2022)

3. Song of Songs- A In-Depth Revelatory Look at the Song of Solomon Verse by Verse!
(2023)

Stay tuned!

R

Refuge Ministries

P.O Box 21

Shortsville, NY 14548

www.findrefuge.tv

Do you have a book in you? NO ONE beats our prices for the value—NO ONE! See the Deeper Life Press website for more!

www.deeperlifepress.com

Deeper Life
PRESS

"Making your book dream come true without robbing you!"
www.deeperlifepress.com

A
B
C
D Direct me .. Deliver me
E
F
G
H
I
J
K
L
M
N
O
P Preserve me Purify me
Q
R Restore me
S
T Teach me / Turn my ♡ toward you
U
V
W
X
Y
Z

Made in the USA
Middletown, DE
09 July 2023

34615128R00165